INTRODUCING DEMOCRACY
80 QUESTIONS
AND ANSWERS

INTRODUCING DEMOCRACY
80 Questions and Answers

David Beetham and Kevin Boyle
with cartoons by Plantu
Second revised edition

UNESCO PUBLISHING

First published in 1995 by the United Nations Educational,
Scientific and Cultural Organization,
7, place de Fontenoy, 75352 Paris 07 SP

ISBN 978-92-3-104087-0

Second revised edition

Typeset by Anne Marie Moncet
Printed by Nouvelle Imprimerie Laballery, Clamecy

Printed in France

Universal Declaration of Human Rights

Article 21

1. Everyone has the right to take part in the government of his country, directly or through freely chosen representatives.

2. Everyone has the right of equal access to public service in his country.

3. The will of the people shall be the basis of the authority of government; this will shall be expressed in periodic and genuine elections which shall be by universal and equal suffrage and shall be held by secret vote or by equivalent free voting procedures.

Note: in the above Declaration 'his' is intended to include 'his or her', which is how it would be expressed today.

Authors' Preface

The first edition of this book was commissioned by UNESCO in 1995 to provide straightforward answers to many of the key questions that people were asking about democracy, both in established democracies and in new and emergent ones. The book was widely acclaimed, and has been translated into some 30 languages. The cartoon illustrations by Plantu, of the French news daily *Le Monde*, gave the work an additional and distinctive attraction.

Much has happened in the world in the decade since the book was first published. There are now more countries recognized as 'democratic' than ever before in the world's history. Yet at the same time there has developed a widespread sense of disillusion with the performance of democracy in practice, and the perception of a growing gulf between people and their elected representatives. New challenges have also emerged which democracies have had to confront: from intensified inequalities within countries and between them; from political corruption and the power of special interests; from the tensions of multicultural and multi-ethnic societies; from religious fundamentalisms; from wars, insurgencies and international terrorism; and from the spread of diseases, including HIV/AIDS. Above all has been the intensification of the processes of globalization, whereby many of the decisions that affect the well-being of a country's population are now beyond the scope of national governments and their democratic procedures.

This new edition reflects these changes and challenges. It also gives a more central place to the human rights which are now recognized as the foundation of democracy: not only the basic civil and political freedoms without which people cannot act politically to express their views, organize collective projects with others or influence the governments which they have elected; but also the necessary economic and social rights without which other freedoms cannot be effectively used and enjoyed.

Of course, many of the key questions that we addressed in the first edition remain as pertinent today as previously. The final statement of the United Nations World Summit in September 2005 included the following: 'We reaffirm that democracy is a universal value ... that while democracies share common features, there is no single model of democracy, that it does not belong to any country or region.' This authoritative and universal declaration also raises many questions in its turn about democracy: what precisely are its values, which are the 'common features' essential to it, and how far do the different practices of each country constitute legitimate variations on this common core. These are some of the central questions which this revised edition seeks to answer, and which are still as relevant today as they were ten years ago.

David Beetham
Kevin Boyle

Contents

3. Free and Fair Elections   59

4. Open and Accountable Government 84

5. Democratic or Civil Society 106

6. The Future of Democracy

1. Basic Concepts and Principles

1. What is democracy?

Throughout our lives we are members of different groups or associations, from families, neighbourhoods, clubs, work-units, to nations and states. In all such associations, from the smallest to the largest, decisions have to be taken for the association as a whole: about the goals to be pursued, about the rules to be followed, about the distribution of responsibilities and benefits between members. These can be called *collective* decisions, in contrast to *individual* decisions taken by people on behalf of themselves alone. Democracy belongs to this sphere of collective decision-making. It embodies the ideal that such decisions, affecting the association as a whole, should be taken by all its members, and that each member should have an equal right to take part in such decisions. Democracy, in other words, entails the twin principles of *popular control* over collective decision-making, and *equality of rights* in the exercise of that control. To the extent that these principles are realized in the decision-making of any association, we can call it democratic.

Democracy in society and state
Defining democracy in this way makes two things clear at the outset. The first is that democracy does not just belong to the sphere of the state or of government, as we usually tend to think of it. Democratic principles are relevant to collective decision-making in any kind of association. Indeed, there is an important relationship between democracy at the level of the state and democracy in the other institutions of society. However, because the state is the most inclusive association, with the right to regulate the affairs of society as a whole, the ability to raise compulsory taxation and the power of lawful punishment over its members, democracy at the level of the state is of crucial importance. It is with democratic government, therefore, that we shall be mostly concerned.

Democracy a matter of degree

The second point about our definition is that democracy is not an all-or-nothing affair, which any actual association either possesses in full or not at all. It is rather a matter of degree: of the extent to which the principles of popular control and political equality are realized, and of greater or lesser approximations towards the ideal of equal participation in collective decision-making. Conventionally we have come to call those states 'democratic' where the government is accountable to the people through competitive election to public office, where all adults have an equal right to vote and to stand for election, and where basic human rights are legally guaranteed. However, in practice, none of these states realizes the two principles of popular control and political equality as fully as it might. To that extent the work of democratization is never ended; and democrats everywhere are involved in struggles to consolidate and extend the realization of democratic principles, whatever regime or political system they happen to live under.

2. Where did the idea of democracy come from?

The idea that ordinary people should be entitled to a say in the decisions that affect their lives is one that has emerged as an aspiration in many different historical societies. It was realized in practice in tribal gatherings in Africa in earlier centuries, in early Middle Eastern popular assemblies, and elsewhere. It achieved a classical institutional form in Athens in the fifth and fourth centuries BCE, from where our term 'democracy' (lit., rule of the people) originated. From the early fifth century onwards, when property qualifications for public office were removed, each Athenian citizen had an equal right to take part in person in discussions and votes in the assembly on the laws and policies of the community, and also to have a share in their administration through jury service and membership of the administrative council, which were recruited in rotation by lot. The example of this working democracy has been a reference point and source of inspiration to democrats ever since. The fact that it coincided with a period of Athenian economic and naval supremacy, and with an enormous flourishing of creative arts and philosophical enquiry, put paid to the idea that giving ordinary people a say in their affairs would produce either a society of drab uniformity or irresponsible government, as the critics of democracy have often asserted.

Direct democracy

Athenian democracy was both more and less democratic than the democracies we know today. It was more democratic in that citizens took part in person in the major decisions of the society ('direct democracy'), whereas today's representative democracies are indirect, and citizens stand at least at one remove from the decision-making processes of government and parliament. For direct democracy to be possible requires a relatively small citizen body capable of being accommodated in a single place of assembly, and one with enough time free from other responsibilities to be able to grasp the evidence and arguments necessary to make an informed political decision. Neither requirement for direct democracy is met by the citizen bodies of today, though there is scope for their involvement in direct decision-making at national level in elections and referenda, and for more continuous participation in decision-making at very local levels, and through the activity of civic associations.

Exclusive citizenship

Athenian democracy was less democratic than those today, however, in that citizenship was restricted to free-born males, excluding women, slaves and resident foreigners. These latter groups ensured the continuity of domestic and productive work necessary to enable the male citizens to engage in political activity. So the active participation of a direct democracy was only possible at all because the citizenship was restricted. 'The people' certainly ruled, but they did so from a position of relative privilege.

Modern exclusivity

It is worth recalling that similar restrictions on citizenship existed in most Western parliamentary systems until well into the twentieth century. The principle made famous by the French Revolution that 'all political authority stems from the people' was not intended to include all the people. Thus it was only in the twentieth century that women and property-less males were granted suffrage; and even today not all adult residents of a country are entitled to vote in its elections, however much they may contribute to its economy.

3. Can a representative system be really democratic?

The eighteenth-century French philosopher Jean-Jacques Rousseau thought not. In a representative system, he argued, people are only free once every few years at election time, when they elect the representatives who are to govern them; thereafter they revert to a position of subordination to their rulers which is no better than slavery. This is an extreme version of the characteristic left-wing or radical critique that representative systems are not properly democratic, because they create a special class of legislators who share a privileged life-style, and come to have different values and interests from the population at large.

Control through election

The simple response is that a representative system is the best system yet devised for securing popular control over government in circumstances where the citizen body is numbered in millions, and has not the time to devote itself continuously to political affairs. The theory is that the people control the government by electing its head (president or prime minister), and by choosing the members of a legislature or parliament which can exercise continuous supervision over the government on the people's behalf, through its power to approve or reject legislation and taxation. This popular control is only effective, however, to the extent that elections are 'free and fair', that government is open, and that parliament has sufficient powers in practice to scrutinize and control its actions (see questions 43, 48 and 54).

Public opinion

Although elections are the major means by which people have a say in government policy in a representative system, they are not the only one. People can join associations to campaign for and against changes in legislation; they can become members of political parties; they can lobby their representatives in person. Governments in turn can be required to consult those affected by their policies, or a selected cross-section of the electorate. Few representative governments in practice are immune to expressions of public opinion such as those regularly provided by opinion polls or through the press, radio and television. Yet all these channels of popular influence are ultimately dependent upon the effectiveness of the electoral process. Governments will only listen seriously to the people when there is a realistic possibility that they will be turned out of office if they do not.

Direct and indirect control

Popular control, then, in a representative system is secured by the direct influence people exercise over the direction of government policy and personnel at elections; through the continuous supervision exercised over government by a representative assembly or parliament; and by the organized expression of public opinion through a variety of channels, which governments have to take into account.

Political equality

What about the second democratic principle, that of political equality? A representative system involves inequality at least in this respect: that it gives a small number of the population the right to take political decisions on behalf of the rest. Within these limits, however, political equality can be achieved to the extent that there is an effective equal right for all citizens to stand for public office, to campaign on public issues, and to obtain redress in the event of maladministration; and that the electoral system gives equal value to each person's vote. Most representative democracies in practice do not fully satisfy these criteria, since political equality is substantially qualified by the systematic differences of wealth, time, access and other resources possessed by different groups of the population. It is one of the tasks of democrats in a representative system to find ways to reduce the political impact of these differences, as well as to make more effective the various mechanisms of popular control over government.

4. Why should we value democracy?

There are many reasons why democracy should be valued, in preference to other types of political system such as monarchy, oligarchy (rule of the few), aristocracy (rule of the best – aristocracies have most often been the rule of the wealthy) and so on. Although some of these systems may have ensured stable rule in the past, none of them meet the criteria which people in a modern society expect from their government – treating all citizens equally, meeting popular needs, resolving differences through discussion and compromise, protecting human rights, and so on. Only democracy can satisfy these criteria.

Equality of citizenship

Democracy aims to treat all people equally. 'Everyone to count for one and none for more than one', wrote the English legal theorist Jeremy Bentham, in his attack on the aristocratic view that some people's lives were intrinsically more valuable than others. The principle of equality requires not only that people's interests be attended to equally by government policy, but that their views should also count equally. 'We give no special power to wealth', spoke an Athenian in one of Euripides' plays; 'the poor man's voice commands equal authority'. Critics of democracy have always objected that the majority is too ignorant, too uneducated and too short-sighted to take any part in determining public policy. To this, democrats answer that the people certainly need information, and the time to make sense of it, but are perfectly capable of acting responsibly when required to do so. Just as we expect all adults to take responsibility for determining their own personal lives, so they are also capable of taking a share in decisions affecting the life of their society.

Meeting popular needs

Democratic government is more likely to meet the needs of ordinary people than other types of government. The more say people have in the direction of policy, the more likely it is to reflect their concerns and aspirations. 'The cobbler makes the shoe,' went the ancient Athenian saying, 'but only the wearer can tell where it pinches'. It is ordinary people who experience the effects of government policy in practice, and it is only if there are effective and consistent channels of influence and pressure from below that government policy will reflect this experience. However well-intentioned the holders of public office may be, if they are immune from popular influence or control, their policies will be at best inappropriate to people's needs, and at worst self-serving and corrupt.

Pluralism and compromise

Democracy relies upon open debate, persuasion and compromise. The democratic emphasis on debate assumes not only that there are differences of opinion and interest on most questions of policy, but that such differences have a right to be expressed and listened to. Democracy thus presupposes diversity and plurality within society as well as equality between citizens. And when such diversity finds expression, the democratic method of resolving differences is through discussion, through persuasion and compromise, rather than by forcible imposition or simple assertion of power. Democracies have often been caricatured as mere 'talking shops'. However, their capacity for public debate should be seen as a virtue rather than a vice, since it is the best means for securing consent to policy, and is not necessarily inconsistent with decisive action. Some democratic theorists speak about 'deliberative democracy' as if it were a particular kind of democracy, when in reality deliberation forms the core of all democratic activity.

Guaranteeing human rights and freedoms

Democracy guarantees human rights and basic freedoms. Open discussion as the method for expressing and resolving societal differences cannot take place without those freedoms that are enshrined in human rights conventions: the rights of free speech and expression, of association with others, of movement, of security for the person. Democracies can be relied upon to protect these rights, since they are so essential to their own mode of existence. Ideally, such rights allow for the personal development of individuals, and produce collective decisions that are better for being tested against a variety of arguments and evidence. At the same time, these rights allow for mistaken or damaging policies of government to be exposed to public view and criticism before they become too entrenched.

Societal renewal

Democracy also allows for societal renewal. By providing for the routine and peaceful removal of policies and politicians that have failed, or outlived their usefulness, democratic systems are able to ensure societal and generational renewal without the massive upheaval or governmental disruption that attends the removal of key personnel in non-democratic regimes.

5. What role do political parties play in a democracy?

Political parties are voluntary associations of like-minded citizens, which campaign to elect their candidates to public office, and to influence or control the personnel and policies of government. Polling surveys show that political parties are the least trusted of all public institutions in almost all countries. Reasons for this will be considered later (see question 44). Here it is worth saying that, if political parties were disbanded, or simply withered away, we should soon find it necessary to reinvent them. This is because, in a large society, people can exercise little public influence as individuals, but only in association with others. Political parties bring together those who share similar views and interests to campaign for political office and influence. They perform a number of different functions. For the *electorate* they help simplify the electoral choice by offering broad policy positions and programmes between which to choose. For *governments* they provide a reasonably stable following of political supporters to enable them to achieve their programme once elected. For the *more politically committed* they provide an opportunity for involvement in public affairs, a means of political education, and a channel for influencing public policy.

Fair competition

In a free and fair electoral system, the success of political parties depends upon the degree of electoral support they can win and maintain. This means that they have to keep in touch with popular opinion in framing their programmes and in selecting candidates for office. If they do not, they will lose out to other parties, or enable new parties to emerge to fill the vacuum. Political parties thus constitute a key mechanism through which popular concerns are made effective in government. They will only fulfil this role, however, to the extent that the electoral competition between them is conducted 'on a level playing field', and that some parties do not have access to government resources or means of communicating with the electorate which others are denied. In particular, this requires that parties in government be made to keep a clear separation between their government and party activities, and between the organizations appropriate to each.

Social division

If open electoral competition between political parties is an indispensable feature of representative democracies, it is also their Achilles' heel. Open competition for government office is socially and politically divisive, and the stakes for those involved are usually high. A condition for democracy's survival, therefore, is that the cost to the losing parties and their supporters in exclusion from office is supportable. In particular, they must have confidence in their ability to fight another electoral contest more successfully, and that their rights to organize, to campaign and to criticize the government will continue unimpaired despite their defeat.

6. Why are the media important to democracy?

All governments, in every type of political system, seek to win the support or acquiescence of the population for their policies. And since a large population can only be reached through the means of mass communication – press, radio and television – these media play a central political role in contemporary societies. In a democracy, however, the media have other important functions than simply to provide a channel for government propaganda. These are to investigate government, to inform the public, to provide a forum for political debate, and to act as a channel for public opinion and popular pressure to reach government.

Journalist as 'watchdog'

The investigative and informative functions of the media are necessary to combat every government's preference for secrecy, and to offset the sheer weight of its public relations machine. A government can only be held publicly accountable if people know what it is doing, and if they have an independent means of testing official claims about its policies. While the media must not overstep the bounds of privacy, it is their task to impart information and a conception of the public interest, and it is the right of the public to receive them. Were it otherwise, the media would be unable to play their vital role of 'public watchdog'.

Public debate

Besides the task of imparting independent information, the media also provide a forum for public debate, through which ministers and other public figures can be interrogated in ways that are accessible

to a mass audience, and that allow for contributions from ordinary citizens. In doing so they also provide a vehicle for the expression of public opinion to government. In all these respects the media serve to complement and reinforce the scrutinizing and deliberative functions of parliament by engaging the population as a whole.

Independence of the media

However, the media can only perform these key democratic tasks if they are properly independent, and not dominated either by government itself or by powerful private interests. The dominance of government can be limited by making publicly financed media accountable to an independent commission or to representatives of citizens' groups, and by allowing competition from privately financed media. The dominance of powerful private interests can be restrained by limiting concentrations of media ownership, and by other forms of regulation. None of these on their own, however, can guarantee that the media fulfil their democratic role impartially and effectively. Ultimately that depends upon the independence and professionalism of journalists, editors and producers themselves, and upon a widespread public acknowledgement of the key contribution that the media make to the democratic process.

7. Why are representative democracies called liberal democracies?

There is first a historical reason. Most Western states became 'liberal' before they became democratic. That is to say they achieved a liberal constitutional order before they granted universal suffrage or developed mass political parties. The key features of such an order were: the subordination of government or executive to the laws approved by an elected parliament (the 'rule of law'); guaranteed rights of the individual to due legal process and to the freedoms of speech, assembly and movement; a judiciary with sufficient independence of both parliament and executive to act as guardians of the law and of these individual rights. Historically, the democracies where suffrage was extended and mass political parties developed without the prior consolidation of these liberal constitutional features have proved very insecure.

The rule of law

This brings us to a second, practical, reason why liberal constitutionalism and democracy belong together. A government in a modern state has enormous powers at its disposal. Whatever its popularity, if the government is not kept subject to the law like everyone else, or if it is not required to seek approval for legislation from parliament according to established procedures, or if it does not respect the liberties of its citizens, however

CHOOSE
YOUR CANDIDATE

PLANTU

unpopular on occasion their exercise may be, then people will rapidly lose the capacity to control it. Democracy is not a system that gives the people whatever they demand at a given moment, or in the shortest possible time, but one which secures the conditions for their influence and control over government on an ongoing basis. And among these conditions are the basic elements of liberal constitutionalism already outlined: the rule of law, the separation of powers between executive, legislature and judiciary, and the guarantee of individual rights and liberties (see questions 20, 52 and 53).

Constitutionalism and democracy

As the term 'constitutionalism' implies, these features, together with the other component elements of democracy, are best protected in a written constitution, in which the rights and duties of citizens, and of the different organs of state, are explicitly defined and publicly known. The special position of the constitution is recognized when public officials are required to swear loyalty to it above party or sectional interest, and by the fact that special measures, such as qualified majorities or referenda, are required to alter it. Yet in practice a written constitution is only secure to the extent that an independent judiciary has the authority and determination to enforce it, and that the public at large is vigilant in its defence.

8. Is liberal democracy the only possible form of democracy?

The twentieth century witnessed a number of attempts to construct democracy at the level of the state without the liberal inheritance, usually in single-party regimes. The most widespread were the Communist systems. Here the argument for the single party was to prevent any reversal in the popular gains of the revolution, to unify society behind a programme of economic development, and to eliminate the influence of private wealth or sectional interests on the political process. The ruling party was intended both as a channel for popular opinion from below and as an instrument for mobilizing the population from above in support of government policy.

Loss of accountability

Undoubtedly there was a certain democratic impetus behind all this, though it is unfashionable now to say so. However, the absence of any freedom of speech and association meant that only those views could be expressed, and only those organizations established, that were approved by the party hierarchy; hence, the influence of citizens over policy and the accountability of public officials to them were severely limited. Despite considerable economic achievements, Communist systems were characterized by authoritarian rule, widespread repression and illegality, and were only able to maintain themselves through the substantial apparatus of a police state.

Single-party rule

A similar, if less extreme, fate met the East African attempts to construct a single-party democracy on non-Communist lines. Here again the intentions were laudable. A single party would prevent the divisiveness of multi-party competition, it was argued, especially in ethnically divided societies, and would reflect the traditional emphasis on consensus, to which the idea of a 'loyal opposition' was quite alien. Moreover, voters would be given a choice between candidates at election time and the chance to remove unpopular ministers, though competition would not go beyond the party and its agreed programme. Once again, however, the inability of people to organize independent of the ruling party, or to oppose it at elections, meant that governments and their leaders became authoritarian and unresponsive, while the lack of any effective separation of powers meant that the rule of law, protection of civil liberties and government accountability through parliament could not be guaranteed.

Liberalism and democracy

The only conclusion that can be drawn from these histories is that attempts to construct democracy without liberalism are doomed to failure. Whatever disadvantages the freedom of association and open electoral competition may have, they have proved an indispensable means to ensure the continuity of popular influence and control over government, while the rule of law and the separation of powers have guaranteed the necessary procedural constraints upon government to make that control effective. In this sense, then democracy at the level of the modern state can only be a 'liberal democracy'. Given these basic elements, however, there is much room for variation around them, according to the distinctive culture and traditions of each country. Democracies vary considerably in practice: in their electoral systems, in the composition of their parliaments, in the way the government is formed, and so on. As the outcome statement of the 2005 United Nations (UN) World Summit declared, 'democracy is a universal value', but 'there is no single model of democracy'.

9. Is a free market economy necessary to democracy?

This is a complex question to which there is no unequivocal answer. On one side, a system of production and distribution based upon the principle of free exchange can be seen as conducive to democracy. Like democracy, the market treats individuals non-paternalistically, as the best judges of their own interests, and as responsible for their own choices. It makes the consumer sovereign in much the same way as the voter is sovereign in a democracy, with the success of firms depending upon the degree of customer support, much as political parties depend upon the degree of electoral support they obtain. Moreover, the market sets limits to the power of the state by decentralizing economic decisions, and by dispersing opportunity, information and resources within civil society. It prevents people from being beholden to the state for their economic destinies, or for the financing of any independent political and cultural activity. In all these ways the market can be seen as supportive of democracy.

Disadvantages of the market

On the other side, however, the market, if left to itself, generates booms and slumps in production which cause enormous economic hardship and dislocation. It makes a country vulnerable to international fluctuations in prices and trade which deprive it of self-determination in its economic policy. Domestically, the market intensifies the disparity in capacity and resources that different economic agents bring to it, in a way that compromises the political equality demanded by democracy. And it treats the labour of workers as just another commodity subject to the laws of supply and demand, to be dispensed with if unwanted, in a manner that is inconsistent with the values that citizenship confers on the individual. It is hardly surprising, therefore, that the early industrializing countries of Western Europe found that the free market was incompatible with a democratic suffrage, which they resisted throughout most of the nineteenth century; or that many subsequent attempts to run a laissez-faire economy have required authoritarian governments to contain popular discontent. Since the Second World War, Western governments have sought to reconcile democracy with a market economy by substantial market regulation and intervention, by economic redistribution, and by creating a system of welfare rights to protect the most vulnerable from the market's vicissitudes, though all these have more recently come under threat.

Ambiguous relationship

Those attracted by the simplicities of laissez-faire would do well to note these ambiguities in the relationship between democracy and the market. The disadvantages have been especially evident in developing countries, which have been exposed to the forces of the international market and the pressures of economic globalization, without the protection for domestic businesses which the advanced economies enjoyed in their own process of development, and which in some sectors they continue to defend. The economic consequences have led to considerable scepticism about free market doctrines and their promotion as a necessary component of democratization (see also questions 67 and 75).

A socialist alternative?

On the other hand, it should be remembered that the centrally planned economies of socialism required an uncontrollable bureaucratic apparatus to administer, allowed the state to absorb all society's energy and initiative, and created huge political inequalities and privileges, none of which were compatible with democracy. Whether a decentralized system of socially-owned enterprises within a market economy could prove either economically workable or consistent with a multi-party democracy remains an unresolved question. The only form of democratic socialism that has so far proved viable in practice has been the social democracy of the Western and Northern European countries since 1945. And that has been more a modification of capitalism than its outright replacement.

10. Is decision by the majority always democratic?

It is a common misconception to equate democracy with majority rule. If we take the term 'democracy' literally as 'rule by the people', then this means rule by the whole people, not by one part of the people over another. In other words, the crucial democratic feature is the right of decision-making which all share equally, whereas decision by the majority is simply a procedural device for resolving disagreement when other methods (discussion, amendment, compromise) have been exhausted. Of course, majority decision must be more democratic than allowing minorities to decide or to obstruct the will of the majority; but in so far as it leaves the minority impotent, without any influence on the outcome, it should be regarded more as a rough and ready device for reaching decision, than the acme of democratic perfection.

Principle of reciprocity

Defenders of majority rule point out that those in the minority on one occasion may always be in the majority on the next, and that their lack of influence in one decision, or in one election, will be compensated by 'winning' later. Minority consent to the majority, in other words, rests upon a norm of reciprocity: their turn to be in the majority will come, and others will have to respect it in the same manner as they have done. However, this principle of reciprocity breaks down if the decision of the majority impairs a minority's capacity to canvass its views in the future; or if the minority is a 'permanent' one; or if the issue being decided is so vital to the minority that it cannot be compensated by winning on different issues in the future. Each of these cases requires separate examination.

Majority and individual rights

Where the decision of a majority (or of a government acting with majority support) infringes the basic human rights necessary to a democracy, it must by definition be undemocratic. These rights are those necessary to enable people to contribute to political life: the freedoms of speech, movement and association; the right to vote and to stand for public office. The guarantee of these rights equally to all citizens constitutes the bedrock of a democratic system; ideally they should be given special protection in a constitution or bill of rights, where they would remain immune from majority infringement. The difficult question of when they can be justifiably suspended or qualified *for everyone* will be discussed later (see questions 23–24).

Permanent minorities

The principle of reciprocity also breaks down where the minority is a 'permanent' one, defined by race, religion, language, ethnicity, or some other permanent characteristic. Where the system of party competition coincides with these communities, rather than cuts across them, such a minority may be permanently excluded from governmental office and from all prospect of political influence. In such a situation the minority may feel that democracy has become, not the rule of the people, but the 'tyranny of the majority'. Various constitutional devices are available to prevent a condition of permanent subordination for such a minority: a system of power-sharing, whereby they are accorded positions in government and other public offices proportionate to their numbers; the right to veto legislation which threatens their vital interests; substantial autonomy in the running of their own affairs. Which of these devices is most appropriate will depend upon the circumstances, for example, whether the minority in question is territorially concentrated or dispersed throughout the country. Whatever the device, however, the right of a people to practise their own culture is now recognized as a basic human right, which requires constitutional protection (see question 26).

Intense minorities

Finally, there is the 'intense' minority. A group may feel that a particular issue is so important to it that impotence in the face of the majority can never be compensated by its being part of a majority on other occasions and on other issues. Such situations simply cannot be legislated for. But a wise majority will go some way towards meeting the minority, if at all possible, rather than using its majority position simply to overrule them. Democracy is only sustainable if people can agree to continue living together. And that requires that majorities, and the governments representing them, be prepared to exercise a measure of self-restraint, and do not always use the majority procedure to capture everything for themselves and their own point of view.

11. Can an individual legitimately disobey the law in a democracy?

Civil disobedience – the public and non-violent breaking of the law in defence of some important principle or vital interest – has an honourable place in the history of democracy. It has been undertaken by men and women to obtain suffrage, to protest against fraudulent elections, to resist compulsory military service, or to campaign against oppressive legislation of all kinds. It is to be distinguished from criminal law-breaking by its openness, political purpose, and the fact that those involved do not seek to evade prosecution or punishment for their offence. Its aim is usually to draw attention to some injustice or outrage perpetrated by public authorities or powerful private bodies, and to compel a rethink of the policy, when other methods of publicity and persuasion have proved ineffective. Less usually, it seeks to make the offending policy unworkable through the organization of mass resistance. However, because it breaks the principle of reciprocity on which consent to the law in a democracy is based (see question 10), it should only be contemplated in exceptional circumstances, and only then as a last resort.

Integrity of the law

Critics of civil disobedience argue that breaking the law can never be justified. The law is the foundation of a civilized society, and disregard for it by one person or group only encourages others to act likewise. If everyone were to pick and choose which laws they were to obey, the framework of law on which we all depend would rapidly disintegrate. Moreover, in a democratic society people have constitutional channels for changing the law: voting in elections, lobbying representatives, legal campaigning to persuade citizens and government of the need to change the offending law or policy. And the very act of taking part in an election indicates consent to the outcome, and agreement to abide by policies that the winning side has campaigned upon. In this view then, civil disobedience is an affront to democracy as well as to the rule of law.

Law and justice

Defenders of the right to civil disobedience point out that consent to abide by the outcome of an election cannot commit a person to obeying every law or cooperating with every policy of government, however unjust it may be. Sometimes the constitutional channels of campaign and protest may simply take too long, while the damage being done is irreversible. In practice, the voices of ordinary people tend to be drowned out by the propaganda of governments and powerful vested interests. In these respects, civil disobedience can serve as a contribution to democracy, rather than its antithesis, by bringing opposition dramatically to public attention. In any case, the final court of decision about right and wrong must be the individual conscience, and no one can evade responsibility for the persistence of unjust laws simply by doing nothing. The historical record suggests that more damage is done by passive acquiescence in the face of oppressive laws than by principled disobedience.

Individual conscience

These differences of view cannot be easily resolved by appeal to general considerations. Much depends upon the precise circumstances of each case, the balance between conflicting principles involved, and an assessment of their respective consequences. Ultimately only individuals can resolve the issue for themselves. One area where the importance of individual conscience is now officially recognized is in the right of conscientious objection to military service; many states are acknowledging the moral force of such objections by making room for alternative forms of service.

12. Is there any connection between nationalism and democracy?

It is often claimed that nationalism and democracy are the chief competing ideologies of the contemporary world. What this claim overlooks is that they share a common historical and ideological origin in the principle of the French Revolution that all political authority stems from the people. The nationalist belief in the self-determination of peoples, each within its own state, is closely akin to the democratic principle that the people of a country should be self-determining in their own affairs. The practical connection between the two was made apparent when the popular pressure that precipitated the end of Communist rule in Eastern and Central Europe produced demands simultaneously for democratic government and for the partition of the former territories into separate nation-states. If the people are to rule, then who constitutes the people becomes a pressing political question.

Nationalism and exclusivity

However, this is not the end of the matter. Whereas democracy is a universalistic doctrine, emphasizing the common human capacity for self-determination which everyone shares despite their differences, nationalism is particularistic, emphasizing differences between peoples, and the value of a nation's distinctive culture, tradition and ways of living. Nationalism tends to be exclusive where democracy is inclusive. And this exclusivity becomes profoundly undemocratic when it leads to the denial of citizenship rights to settled residents in a territory, simply because they do not share the language, religion or ethnic origins of the most numerous national group. If all states coincided neatly with a single homogeneous people or nation there would be no problem. In reality, however, centuries of migration and conquest have so intermingled the peoples of the world that the concept of the nation-state as the home of a single national or ethnic grouping is nowhere to be realized.

Nationalism and democratic rights

Although national demands for self-determination can therefore be seen as consistent with democratic principles, the denial of equal political rights to settled residents, or the refusal to grant any autonomy to minority peoples within the territory, must be judged undemocratic. Moreover, in view of the manifest potential of such denials to disrupt the peace, both within and between states, they cannot simply be regarded as an internal matter, to be decided by the country in question. Basic democratic rights, as a part of human rights, are now regarded as a common property and legitimate aspiration of all humankind; and their denial is regarded as a proper ground for concern, and even (where appropriate) of sanction, on the part of the international community. The particularism of nationhood and ethnicity, in other words, can now only be legitimately asserted on the basis of acknowledging our common humanity, and not at its expense.

13. How is a transition to democracy brought about?

The concept of democratic transition denotes a political process whereby a non-democratic regime comes to be replaced by one based on competitive elections and universal suffrage. The historical record indicates that democracy is rarely established in any country without widespread popular struggle and mobilization, sometimes over a lengthy period and at considerable personal cost. Ordinary people have to be convinced of the necessity of democratic government to the realization of their basic aspirations, and must organize to demand it. In other words, democracy does not come handed down from above. Traditional rulers, military dictators, Communist apparatchiks, life presidents, foreign occupiers – none of them give up power voluntarily, but only when their regime has become widely discredited, and popular mobilization has convinced them that their continuation in power can only provoke deepening disorder and ungovernability, as in the so-called 'velvet revolutions' in Eastern Europe in 1989–90.

Three waves of democracy

It is now a common practice, following Samuel Huntington, to identify three periods or 'waves' of democratization in the twentieth century. The first wave had gained its impetus from the American and French Revolutions, and reached its climax after the end of the First World War with the introduction of democracy and universal suffrage in many European countries. There followed a 'reverse wave' from the 1920s onwards as many countries embraced fascism or reverted to authoritarian rule. A second wave took place after the end of the Second World War, with the restoration of democracy in much of Europe, its introduction or re-introduction in many countries of Latin America, and its establishment in many countries of Asia and Africa as they gained their independence from the colonial powers. Again this was followed by a second 'reverse wave' from the 1960s onwards. The third wave began with the return to democracy in Portugal, Spain and Greece from 1974 onwards, gradually extended to many countries of Latin America and Asia during the 1980s, and was given an enormous impetus by the 'velvet revolutions' which brought Communist rule to an end in Europe, and by the success of liberation struggles in southern Africa. So far, with the exception of one or two countries, a feared third 'reverse wave' has failed to materialize, though much still needs to be done to strengthen the democracies that have been established.

14. How can democracy be established in post-conflict situations?

A special challenge exists in countries where democracy comes to be established in the aftermath of civil war or an armed liberation struggle. Here the challenge is not only to fashion democratic institutions, but also to establish what could be called the pre-conditions for democracy: a minimally effective state whose authority reaches across the territory, and some sense of common nationhood. Yet democratic processes can also powerfully assist the realization of these pre-conditions, in so far as they substitute negotiation and dialogue for force and coercion, and give all parties to a conflict a sense of inclusion and a stake in a future government. Only such processes can secure societal legitimacy for a new political order, and hence respect for its authority across the country's territory. An institution that has proved effective in many post-conflict situations has been the 'truth and reconciliation commission', by means of which families of victims can ascertain the fate of their loved ones and obtain a public acknowledgment of responsibility. Some take the view, however, that, in such commissions, considerations of justice may be too readily sacrificed to the need for reconciliation.

International support

Support from democracies abroad can assist considerably in both attaining victory for democratic forces and establishing a democratic constitution. During the Cold War, however, Western democracies were more interested in limiting the spread of Communism in other countries than in encouraging democracy, and to this end they helped maintain some highly undemocratic regimes in power. Since the end of the Cold War, the balance of international activity has shifted decisively towards supporting democratic movements and governments (see question 76). Although such support is important, it can be no substitute for a people's own struggle against authoritarian rule. After all, there is something self-contradictory about a country having self-government imposed upon it from outside; and in any case such a regime is unlikely to last for long.

15. Once achieved, how can democracy be maintained?

There is no simple recipe. The Western democracies only achieved stability over a long period of time, and after experiencing periodic reversals at the hands of aristocratic reaction, military dictatorship, or fascism. In some of the recently established democracies, circumstances may seem quite unfavourable for democratic sustainability. Thus social divisions may run too deep to be accommodated within a free political order. Or the economy may be too impoverished to enable legitimate popular expectations to be met. Or the military may be too powerful and too unreconciled to a non-political role.

Democratic consolidation
However, it is mistaken to imagine that people are powerless in the face of unfavourable conditions. Measures can be taken to consolidate democratic institutions so as to withstand the pressures to which they will inevitably be subject. Much depends, for example, on the quality and training of the professionals who occupy key roles within the state: the judiciary and constitutional lawyers, parliamentary clerks, election officers and the civil service more widely. Political parties need to be built up, and to have access to training for their own cadres. Key institutions of civil society – the media, businesses, trade unions, non-governmental organizations (NGOs) – need to develop the capacity to act independently of the state and its tutelage. Much also depends upon the ability and integrity of top political leaders, and their commitment to democratic and constitutional politics, as well as to the solution of immediate problems and the continuation of their own power.

Two-sided struggle
The maintenance of democracy can perhaps best be seen as a campaign waged on two fronts simultaneously. On one side is

the struggle against anti-democratic forces, which may never have reconciled themselves to free institutions or to the influence of ordinary people on the political process. On the other side is a struggle to contain the divisive features of democratic politics itself, such as the competition for government office, and the temptation to treat politics as a game in which the winners take all the prizes. The first struggle will depend upon the breadth of the institutions and groups within society which have an interest in the survival of democracy, and a readiness to defend it. The second will depend upon a certain self-restraint in the exercise of power and a willingness to keep open the dialogue with political opponents, as well as upon respect for the political rights of others on the part of the population at large.

Second 'velvet revolutions'

In a number of post-Communist countries, such as Serbia-Montenegro (in 2000), Georgia (2003) and Ukraine (2004), it has required a second popular uprising in protest at a fraudulent or 'stolen' presidential election to lay a secure basis for a democratic political system. Here and elsewhere, the authoritarian style of rule typical of the former Communist party-state had been perpetuated under the mantle of supposedly free elections and multi-party competition. In these countries, the refusal of the armed forces to intervene to break up the popular protests made a significant contribution to a peaceful outcome. In each country also, the role of the national parliament was important in helping resolve the crisis, and in modifying the 'super-presidential' form of government in a more parliamentary direction.

16. What are the chief components of a functioning democracy?

There are four main components or building blocks of a functioning democracy. These are: human rights and fundamental freedoms; free and fair elections; open and accountable government; a democratic or 'civil' society. These components have been touched on in the answers to previous questions; here they will be outlined more systematically, since they provide the framework for the following sets of questions. This framework can be represented diagrammatically as a 'democratic pyramid', in which each component is necessary to the whole (see Figure 1). A glance at this pyramidal structure should make clear that democracy cannot be equated merely with electoral democracy or indeed any other single component.

Human rights and fundamental freedoms

Human rights encompass those basic rights and freedoms – of expression, association, movement, and so on – which are a necessary condition for people to act politically, whether in terms of self-organization within civil society, or to bring influence to bear upon government. Although these rights are properly guaranteed to *individuals*, as a part of human rights more generally, their value lies in the context of *collective* action: joining with others for common ends, campaigning, influencing public opinion, etc. It is thus mistaken to see individual rights as necessarily antithetical to collective purposes, or to the processes of collective decision-making and their popular control, for which they constitute rather the necessary foundation. It is also now increasingly accepted that, without the basic economic and social rights which guarantee the means to a healthy life and the education necessary for it, these fundamental freedoms cannot be effectively exercised.

Figure 1. The democratic pyramid

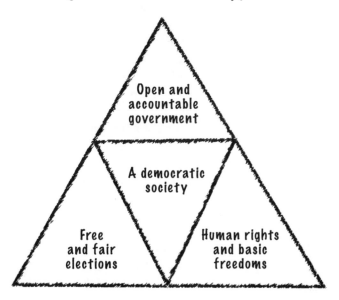

Free and fair elections

Competitive elections are the key device whereby public officials are rendered accountable and subject to popular control. They also constitute an important arena for ensuring political equality between citizens, both in access to public office and in the value of their votes. The criterion of 'free and fair elections' embraces in the first place the electoral *system*, i.e. the laws governing which offices are electable, who may stand for them, when elections are to be held, who may vote, how constituencies are to be defined, how votes are aggregated to select the winners, and so on. Second is the electoral *process*, i.e. how individual elections are conducted in practice, from the initial registration of voters through the campaign to the counting of the ballots, to ensure that the law is strictly and impartially applied, and that there is no malpractice which may throw the result into question.

Open and accountable government

The accountability of government to the public in a democracy is on the one side a *legal* accountability: to the courts for the observance of the law by all public officials (the 'rule of law'); on the other side a *political* accountability: to parliament and the public for the justifiability of government policy and actions. This accountability depends upon the independence from government, respectively, of the courts in their power to defend the constitution, to determine guilt and to punish offences; and of parliament in its powers of legislation, taxation and scrutiny of government. This independence of the courts and parliament from the government or executive is what is meant by the term 'separation of powers'. Besides being accountable, democratic government should also be responsive, both through formal requirements of consultation, and through its openness to the expression of public opinion in its various forms.

A democratic or 'civil' society

The idea of 'civil' society indicates the necessity to democracy of having social associations of all kinds that are organized *independently* of the state. Only in this way can the power of the state be limited, can public opinion be articulated from below rather than managed from above, and can society achieve the self-confidence to resist arbitrary rule. The principle that such associations should be not only independent but also *internally democratic* embodies the idea that democracy at the level of the state will only be weakly rooted if the rest of society is run on autocratic lines. If people are conditioned to authoritarianism in the family, the school and the church, and if they have no experience of self-organization or co-determination in the workplace, the neighbourhood and voluntary associations, they are unlikely to prove active citizens, or feel any responsibility for the condition of their society at large.

2. Human Rights and Fundamental Freedoms

17. What are human rights?

Human rights and fundamental freedoms are individual entitlements derived from human needs and capacities. The recognition of human rights and the creation of means for their defence in international law constitute perhaps the most important moral advance of the twentieth century. The international community has adopted many international agreements or conventions on human rights. These instruments seek to establish agreed definitions about the scope of human rights and freedoms and at the same time commit governments to take the necessary steps to ensure that such rights are protected in law and practice in their respective countries. These rights and freedoms constitute an essential building block of democracy (see questions 20–22).

The Universal Declaration

The main source of human rights ideas in the modern world is the Universal Declaration of Human Rights, adopted by the United Nations (UN) General Assembly on 10 December 1948. In 1966, the UN adopted two international instruments based on the rights proclaimed in the Universal Declaration. These are the International Covenant on Economic Social and Cultural Rights and the International Covenant on Civil and Political Rights. To date, all but about 40 of the 192 UN member states have ratified these instruments. Thus the great majority of governments in the world undertake to report periodically to monitoring committees on how they are securing the human rights of their populations. Under an Optional Protocol to the International Civil and Political Covenant, individuals have a right to complain to the monitoring body for this Covenant, the Human Rights Committee, if their rights have been violated by their governments. But this right is available only if the state in question has accepted this Protocol. So far over 110 states have done so. A parallel complaint procedure for the International Covenant on Economic, Social and Cultural Rights is established by the Optional Protocol thereto adopted on 10 December 2008 by the UN General Assembly (its entry into force requires ten ratifications). The Universal Declaration of Human Rights and the two Covenants are together known as the International Bill of Rights. There are also many other human rights treaties agreed by states through the United Nations. The Convention on the Rights of the Child is the most ratified of all human rights treaties, and 185 states have ratified the Women's Convention which requires them to eliminate discrimination against women in the enjoyment of all their rights.

Regional Conventions

There are also regional human rights treaties, but not all world regions have human rights systems. At present only Africa, the Americas and Europe have them. The African Charter on Human and Peoples Rights was adopted in 1981, the American Convention on Human Rights in 1969 and the European Convention on Human Rights in 1950. There are continuing efforts to strengthen human rights protection at regional and sub-regional levels in the Asia Pacific region, including Arab countries. (Suggestions for further reading on regional human rights protection systems can be found at the end of the book.)

18. How are rights classified?

Rights can be classified in many ways but the most accepted is into civil, political, social, economic and cultural rights. This is the classification adopted in the International Bill of Human Rights. Examples of civil and political rights are: the right to life; freedom from torture; freedom from forced labour; freedom from arbitrary arrest; the right to fair trial; freedom of thought, conscience, religion or belief; the right to private life; the freedoms of speech and association; and the right to take part in public affairs. Civil and political rights are typically rights which require the state to refrain from action or interference with individuals or groups, for example, by not unjustly arresting and detaining people or subjecting them to torture. But the state has positive duties also. It must establish a police force in order to protect people from crime. It must fund a legal aid system to ensure that the poor can defend their rights in court when they face serious criminal charges. Another example would be the positive duty to make and implement laws to prevent discrimination on grounds such as racial or ethnic origins, sex or religion.

Economic, social and cultural rights

Examples of economic, social and cultural rights are the rights to food and to health, to an adequate standard of living, to work, to equal pay for equal work, to strike, to form trade unions, to social security, to housing, to education, and to participate in cultural life. The obligation to 'respect, protect and fulfil' these rights may require a state to act as provider, where individuals cannot provide for themselves, for example because they are unemployed or homeless, or because they are disabled. Under the International Covenant on Social Economic and Cultural Rights, states have an obligation to take steps to 'progressively realize' certain of these rights over time. There is a recognition that, for example, to ensure to an adequate standard the right to education, or health for all, needs time as well as the commitment of significant resources. Other rights, for example trade union rights and freedom from discrimination, should be implemented fully and without delay.

No rights more important than others

All internationally recognized human rights are interrelated and reinforce each other (see question 19). In some societies, depending on their stage of development, certain rights may be taken for granted by most citizens: for example, in richer countries the right to a reasonable standard of living, and the rights to food, clothing, shelter and education. In poorer countries these rights will be uppermost in the concerns of the people. But in all democratic societies such economic and social rights are fundamental and should be guaranteed without discrimination, just as basic civil and political rights, the right to be governed under the rule of law, to have protection from arbitrary arrest and detention, and to enjoy freedom of expression and the right to political participation are fundamental and should be guaranteed to all.

Freedom from discrimination

Human rights are the entitlements of everyone everywhere on an equal basis. The individual has a right to equal treatment with others. Thus, an important principle attached to all rights is that in exercising them people should not be discriminated against on grounds such as sex, race, religion or belief.

19. Are human rights universal?

Here is how the international community meeting in Vienna in 1993 answered this question:

> All human rights are universal, indivisible and interdependent and interrelated. The international community must treat human rights globally in a fair and equal manner, on the same footing, and with the same emphasis. While the significance of national and regional particularities and various historical, cultural and religious backgrounds must be borne in mind, it is the duty of States, regardless of their political, economic and cultural systems, to promote and protect all human rights and fundamental freedoms (Vienna Declaration and Programme of Action Article 5).

The answer, therefore, is yes. International human rights standards address common human needs and capacities of the individual everywhere in the world. But they also recognize that, while we are all entitled to be treated equally, we are also all different. The world is made up of different regions and cultures. It is also divided between poorer and richer countries. It has been argued that the international human rights standards, because they begin with the individual, are alien to cultures which do not see the individual separate from the community or which emphasize the duty of the individual to community first. Whether contemporary ideas of individual human rights are causing societies to reinterpret the relationship between communities and their members is a subject that is much debated, both in the North as well as the South. The answer is probably yes, but there is no evidence that the recognition or the protection of individual human rights damages human solidarity and community. To the contrary, the norms of universal human rights seek to protect human groups and peoples and recognize the need for individuals to join with others, in the use of their own language, to belong to and to participate in their own cultures, religions and ways of life. International human rights law recognizes first a basic level of common entitlements to human rights of all human beings, but beyond that accepts and endorses the entitlement of all cultures to flourish, including those of indigenous peoples. The importance of sustaining cultural diversity in a world of global communications and unprecedented mobility of people led UNESCO to adopt the Universal Declaration on Cultural Diversity in 2001 and the Convention on the Protection and Promotion of the Diversity of Cultural Expressions in 2005.

Rights and duties

Just because human rights are universal in principle does not mean that they are universally enjoyed. They are not. The Universal Declaration of Human Rights makes it the task of everyone to work for universal rights in practice and not just in theory. The Universal Declaration also speaks of the individual's duties to his or her community. It asserts that an individual's free and full development of personality is only possible in community with others. The notion of human rights nevertheless begins with the belief in the unique worth of every individual human person. (See also question 4).

2005 United Nations World Summit

These important understandings about human rights and the duties of the international community were confirmed at a Summit of Heads of States and Governments held at the United Nations (UN) in September 2005. The Summit confirmed the universality of all rights, the duty of all states to actively promote and protect them and the responsibility of the international community to protect civilians at risk. It also declared that all rights are interdependent, and that human rights, the rule of law and democracy 'belong to the universal and indivisible core values and principles of the United Nations'.

20. What is the relation between human rights and democracy?

The 2005 World Summit spoke of the relation between human rights and democracy (along with that of development) as being 'interdependent and mutually reinforcing'. Another way of expressing this point is that it is now recognized by the international community that the protection of human rights

and the rule of law, not only in developed but also in developing states, is best achieved through a commitment to democratic principles. It is also recognized that the exercise of human rights and freedoms is necessary for democracy to properly function at all. It used to be claimed that individual human rights could be defended and enjoyed in undemocratic systems, especially where the priority had to be given to economic development. But the evidence is overwhelming that such systems become, sooner rather than later, less benign, more repressive, corrupt and unstable.

Democratic government as a human right

The belief in the intimate relationship between democracy and human rights is not new. The Universal Declaration of Human Rights included an endorsement of democratic government. It states as one of its ideals that 'the will of the people shall be the basis of the authority of government' (Article 21). The International Covenant on Civil and Political Rights requires states to guarantee for every citizen the right and opportunity to ... 'take part in the conduct of public affairs, directly or indirectly through chosen representatives, to vote and to be elected at genuine periodic elections [and] to have access on general terms of equality to public office' (Article 25). The 2005 UN World Summit described democracy as a universal value. While acknowledging that democracies share common features, the world's governments also agreed that there is no single model of democracy, and that democracy does not belong to any one country or region.

Right to development

The unambiguous acknowledgment of the interdependent relation between the idea of universal human rights and that of democratic government is among the most important advances in international relations since the end of the Cold War. Equally, the general acceptance by the developing world of respect for human rights and democratic government as the basis for the achievement of the right to development, has been a further positive advance in this period. Development is only sustainable in the long term if people can participate in shaping development policies, and if development programmes are accountable to the people and are pursued within a framework which respects all human rights and the rule of law.

21. What is the relation between civil and political rights and democracy?

The guarantee of civil and political rights for the individual citizen plays a dual role in democracy. First, these rights are essential for securing the twin democratic principles of popular control and political equality in collective decision-making. Secondly, such rights and freedoms act as a constraint on collective action by defining spheres of individual freedom and choice, which are outside the reach of majority decision. This dual role is best illustrated by examining briefly some of the civil and political rights most intimately linked with the democratic system.

Liberty and security of the person

Without protection from arbitrary arrest, detention, banishment or expulsion, the individual cannot with security participate in political debate or action. This common-sense point is illustrated by the rule that members of the legislature are normally immune from arrest while engaged in parliamentary duties. But the need

for respect for the right to liberty extends to all in a democracy. A democratic society defends the liberty and physical integrity of the unpopular individual, for example, even against the wishes of a majority.

'Due process'

Similar arguments can be made for the need to protect the citizen from unfair accusation, ill treatment and torture, and a biased trial. To prosecute political enemies is commonplace in societies which reject democracy. A democratic society requires an independent judiciary, a properly trained and paid police service and an administration of criminal justice which is based on the rule of law and devoid of political and ideological influence, manipulation and corruption.

Freedom of thought and conscience

A democratic society presupposes that each individual is free to think as he or she wishes and to hold his or her own ideas, opinions and general philosophy of life. Equally, a democratic society offers freedom for the individual to adhere, along with others, to a religion or belief and to practise and manifest beliefs, subject only to the rights of others. Freedom of thought must always be protected as an individual right against what may be the prevailing and even the overwhelming majority's beliefs, whether of a religious or secular nature. In particular, minorities of different religions or beliefs are entitled to the same guarantees of freedom as the majority community.

Freedom of expression and the media

The essence of democracy as we have defined it has been that each citizen has a voice equally entitled to be heard. Freedom of speech is therefore an essential human right, if each citizen is to have the opportunity to be heard. The international standards on freedom of speech concern not only the right to speak out but also the right 'to seek and to receive information and ideas of all kinds, through any media regardless of frontiers'. Thus the mass media should be independent of government control and – within clear rules established to protect individuals' reputation and privacy – free to inform the citizen, to criticize the government and to stimulate all manner of debate on policy choices (see question 6). The internet should also be free from government or corporate interference and accessible to all. These freedoms also carry with them responsibilities, for example, not to gratuitously offend religious or other sensibilities, especially when the offended group constitutes a minority or marginalized group.

Freedom of information

The openness of government in a democracy is enhanced by the principle of freedom of information, that is, that government information and documentation are freely accessible to the public and, subject to narrow exceptions, are not classified as confidential or secret. (See question 49).

Freedom of assembly and association

The modern representative democracy could not function without guarantees that people are free to come together to discuss public affairs, to form trade unions and other associations, to press their interests with government and to form and participate in political parties. These freedoms include the right to congregate, to demonstrate, and to petition for the redress of grievances.

22. How do economic, social and cultural rights relate to democracy?

In the 'democratic pyramid' (see question 16), the fundamental rights which secure employment, housing, food, an adequate living standard, education, and other needs, are treated as the essential foundation of civil society. A society where there is widespread hunger can only achieve democratic politics very imperfectly. The satisfaction of basic human needs to survive is a necessary basis for democracy to function. Democratic principles require that each elector or citizen should have an equal voice. To the extent that there is gross inequality in life chances, and in access to education for example, the democratic potential of a society is severely limited. At the same time, democracy as a collective process is a means whereby such inequalities can be identified and alleviated.

23. Are there grounds on which a democratic government can legitimately limit rights?

International standards permit restriction of the exercise of certain rights on specific grounds, such as public order, public morals, national security and the rights of others. However, certain rights may not be so restricted. Certain fundamental guarantees of the individual, such as freedom from torture, freedom of thought and freedom from discrimination, may never be withdrawn in a democratic society.

Principles governing rights restrictions

The principles concerning the justification of an interference with, or restriction of, a right are well established in international jurisprudence. These are: that the restriction is provided for by law; that it pursues a legitimate aim, in other words that the purpose of the limitation is clearly one permitted by international law; and that the necessity for the interference or limitation can be justified on democratic principles. In practice, this last test means that a government must show that its actions in limiting a right or freedom are proportionate and not excessive. An example of justified limitation on an individual's freedom of speech would be where this freedom is deliberately used to incite violence or hatred towards others because of their ethnic origins, colour or religious beliefs. But to suppress a political party can never be justified except in the clearest case when an organization has become involved in unconstitutional or violent actions. Equally, it is only in rare circumstances that international human rights standards would countenance prior censorship of the press. Such an exception might be a newspaper's intention to publish highly sensitive information and where a court is satisfied that publication would put lives in immediate danger or would threaten the security of the country.

24. Can human rights be suspended in an emergency?

International human rights standards permit the temporary suspension of guarantees of certain civil and political rights in circumstances of a public emergency which 'threatens the life of the nation' and which is officially proclaimed. The most frequently invoked justification by governments for resort to emergency powers is the existence of internal political or ethnic conflict which has developed into violence and terrorism. Typically, police or other security forces are given additional powers of arrest, and search and detention without trial may be introduced. Powers to record private telephone conversations or to retain email records as counter-terrorism measures are other current examples. But the exercise of such powers must go along with strict safeguards, and any abuses must be punished.

Non-derogable rights

A democratic society will resort to emergency powers with reluctance and implement the principle of exercising special powers to the minimum extent necessary, for the shortest period necessary, and with the maximum safeguards against abuse. Even in an emergency there are certain rights which may not be suspended (or derogated from), for instance, the right to life, freedom of thought and conscience, and freedom from torture. These are known as 'non-derogable rights' and are to that extent absolute rights and freedoms. The ignoring by governments of such principles is widespread today and represents a great threat to democratic societies. The so-called 'war on terrorism', pursued by some governments as if it were a permanent state of emergency, has proved particularly damaging to fundamental freedoms. Kofi Annan, then UN General-Secretary, warned against this in a prophetic speech in November 2001: 'The danger is that in pursuit of security we end up sacrificing crucial liberties, thereby weakening our common security, not strengthening it – and thereby corroding the vessel of democratic government from within.'

25. Can a democracy legitimately exclude anyone from citizenship?

The answer is that a state has, in principle, the right to determine who may become a member or citizen and how citizenship rights are acquired. But in the exercise of these sovereign powers a state must not behave in an arbitrary way, for example by operating a racially discriminatory immigration policy.

Rights of resident non-citizens

International human rights law generally requires the equal treatment of citizens and non-citizens. A state may deny political rights to resident non-citizens, although the trend in democratic practice is to offer rights of political participation, including voting rights, following a reasonable period of residence (see question 34). But, apart from the political rights which go with citizenship, the state is obliged to ensure that non-citizens have all other basic rights and freedoms protected without distinction or discrimination. Laws providing for the obtaining of citizenship must not discriminate between individuals who seek citizenship on such grounds as their ethnic or racial origin, colour, descent, culture or religion.

Migrant workers

Our globalized world is characterized today by the massive migration of people in search of a better life. UN research has shown that one in every fifty human beings is a migrant worker, a refugee or asylum seeker, or an immigrant living in a 'foreign country'. Money transfers made by such workers to their countries of origin account for much greater resources than the sum of all development aid. As a result of migration, many societies have become multi-ethnic in character, and have gained in strength and prosperity. But some societies are less successful in accommodating newcomers and their descendants, leading to xenophobia, violence and discrimination against them (see question 70).

A democratic approach

The democratic approach to migration is one based on a positive policy of managed legal migration that is understood and accepted by the electorate, and that ensures protection of migrants from discrimination and exploitation, including those who have entered the country by irregular means. All governments should cooperate to stop migrant smuggling by organized criminal groups. All countries should become parties to the UN International Convention on the Protection of the Rights of All Migrant Workers and Members of their Families.

Asylum seekers

Asylum seekers and refugees are an exceptional category of migrants who have the right to seek asylum from persecution in another country. The state has a duty to consider their claim fairly under the international laws governing the protection of refugees, and to refuse to return refugees to countries where their lives or freedom would be threatened.

26. What rights do minorities have in a democracy?

International human rights norms offer specific guarantees for minority communities, whether defined as religious, cultural, national, ethnic or linguistic minorities. Such minorities are entitled not only to have the state recognize their existence, but also to have it protect their specific cultural identity and to encourage conditions for the promotion of that identity. Persons belonging to minorities have full democratic rights including the right to participate on equal terms with others in the affairs of the country, as well as to participate in decisions which affect their particular communities or the regions in which they live.

UN Declaration on Minorities

These and other principles are set out in the United Nations Declaration on the Rights of Persons Belonging to National or Ethnic, Religious and Linguistic Minorities, adopted by the General Assembly of the United Nations in December 1992. Many if not most states have minority communities, and it should be a test of a democratic society that it has a positive approach to the rights of a minority. Implementing the principles of this UN Declaration should be a clear and urgent objective for all countries. Implementation of the UNESCO Universal Declaration on Cultural Diversity and its Action Plan would be equally positive for minorities and for social cohesion (see question 19).

27. How are human rights to be defended in practice?

Democratic societies will differ on the means they devise for the protection of rights. However, international standards offer some guidelines, including the requirement that every individual must have a remedy when a violation of rights is alleged. Individuals should be able to invoke their rights in court under those international treaties on human rights which their governments have agreed to. All but a few states in the world have written constitutions in which human rights commitments are defined and guaranteed alongside the processes of the democratic system itself. Typically the courts are in the front line in defence of the individual's rights as defined in the constitution's 'Bill of Rights'. Individuals should have unimpeded access to court, including (if necessary) legal aid, to vindicate their rights. And the judgements and directions of the courts should be implemented by the government; this implementation should include, if the constitution so provides, the rescinding of laws and the payment of compensation. However, the protection of rights often requires positive action as well through the adoption of legislative and other measures, to ensure for example the outlawing of all forms of discrimination and the securing of basic entitlements to vulnerable groups including children, the socially disadvantaged and the disabled.

Unelected judges vs. elected politicians

But is it 'undemocratic', as some would assert, if judges who are typically non-elected act to frustrate the measures of a lawfully elected government? Not if they are acting to protect those basic rights necessary to the exercise of equal citizenship, or to ensure that government itself keeps within its legally defined powers (see 'rule of law', question 53). Not everything that an elected government does is necessarily 'democratic', just because it has a broad democratic legitimacy deriving from the electoral process. Elected governments can act arbitrarily, in a discriminatory way, or even oppressively; and the courts can provide an essential democratic corrective.

Other institutions for defending rights

In a democracy, people turn often to their elected representatives for help in securing justice and their entitlements. The media can equally be of pivotal importance as a watchdog on the abuse of rights. In practice, a range of institutions are deployed in the defence of rights, including, for example, a national human rights institution or an ombudsman to oversee the operation of government administration. But the best defence of democracy is belief in its principles and purposes. Therefore education at all levels in human rights and democratic citizenship is essential. Education programmes should not be confined to schools and colleges but should extend to public authorities including such agencies as the police and military.

International protection
International and regional instruments also contribute to the defense of human rights through their monitoring bodies and by providing complaint procedures (see question 17). In addition, the practice of appointing experts (special rapporteurs/representatives) to study and report on issues or countries of concern enables international and regional organizations to influence governments and to work with them to improve the protection of human rights.

28. Is expression of international concern over a country's human rights record legitimate?

One commitment democratic states make is to accept criticism of their human rights record both from their own population and from the international community. The principle of non-interference in the internal affairs of states by other states is one of the cardinal principles of the modern international order as laid down in the Charter of the United Nations. However, the growth of the international human rights movement and the steady extension of international human rights standards have brought about a new position: how any state treats its citizens is in the international public domain, and external criticism from other governments or NGOS does not constitute interference in the internal affairs of that country.

Non-selective standards
But criticism by other states should be even-handed and not selective. Too often, states condemn the human rights abuses of their opponents and overlook the record of their allies or of those with whom they wish to do business. If universal support for human rights and democracy is to be achieved, an international order based on respect for human rights must be based on a system of common global standards with full international accountability required of all countries.

Responsibility to protect

An important new doctrine in international law is called the responsibility to protect. UN member states have a collective responsibility to protect civilians against international crimes of genocide, war crimes, ethnic cleansing and crimes against humanity. This arises when a country is unable or unwilling to protect its own people. It will be for the UN Security Council to decide how to act, including by intervention in the country. In addition, an International Criminal Court came into existence in 2002 with a mandate to prosecute individuals, including military and government officials, who are accused of such international crimes.

3. Free and Fair Elections

29. Why are elections important?

Elections constitute the key democratic device whereby citizens choose between candidates for public office, and authorize those elected to act on the public's behalf during their period of office. The purpose of elections at national level is twofold. First is to

choose the head of government or chief executive, and the broad policy which the government will pursue. Second is to choose the members of the representative assembly, legislature or parliament, who will decide on legislation and taxation, and scrutinize the work of government on the people's behalf. In a *presidential* system, where the president is the head of government, these two purposes are clearly distinguished by having separate elections for president and members of the legislature, respectively; such elections may or may not take place at the same time. In a *prime-ministerial* or *parliamentary* system, one set of elections will fulfil both purposes, since it is the elected members of parliament who will determine the head of government on the basis of which party leader can win majority support in parliament.

Elections and popular control

The regular election of these public officials by universal suffrage in an open and competitive process constitutes the key instrument of popular control in a representative democracy. Elections demonstrate that political power derives from the people and is held in trust from them; and that it is to the people that politicians must account for their actions. In the last resort it is only the possibility of being turned out of office which ensures that those elected fulfil their trust and maintain the standards of public office, and which guarantees those changes in the personnel and policies of government that changing circumstances require.

Why the ballot should be secret

The English liberal philosopher John Stuart Mill believed that voting should be carried out in public, so that electors would be answerable to their fellow citizens for the way they cast their vote, and so be encouraged to consider the wider public interest rather than their narrow private interest. Few later thinkers have endorsed this rather lofty view. In practice, public voting renders electors vulnerable to improper pressure from the powerful – employers, landowners, priests, superiors of all kinds – and to systematic bribery from those seeking election. The secret ballot, whereby mechanisms are in place to ensure that no one else can know which candidate(s) any elector has voted for, is now established as a central feature of all democratic systems.

30. Should the Head of State be popularly elected?

The office of Head of State is primarily a ceremonial and symbolic one, representing the unity of the nation above the competition of party, the continuity of the state above the changeability of governments, and the permanence of the constitution above the temporality of particular legislation. This symbolic function can attain a special importance at moments of national crisis or constitutional controversy, when the Head of State may come to exercise considerable discretionary power.

Different systems

Different kinds of political system have very different ways of selecting the Head of State. In a presidential system (see question 29), the elected president combines the ceremonial function of Head of State with the executive function of head of government (as in the Russian Federation, the United States, and most Latin American countries), and it may not always be easy to distinguish the two functions. In a parliamentary system (see question 29), the Head of State is a completely separate office from that of the prime minister, who leads the government. Here the Head of State may take the form of a non-executive president, chosen by parliament or by direct election of the people (Germany, Ireland, India, etc.). Or it may take the form of a constitutional monarch, where the Head of State is determined by birth and will typically hold office for life (as in Japan, Thailand, Spain, etc.) There is no simple answer as to which of these is best, since each has to be assessed in the context of the constitutional system as a whole.

31. What other public offices should be popularly elected?

Since the elected chief executive is responsible to the public and to parliament for the conduct and competence of all civil servants in the employ of national government, there is a strong argument for making such posts subject to appointment from above rather than election from below, provided the initial recruitment to them is open to any qualified member of society. However, a democracy also requires public services that are responsive to *local* needs and to the variability of local circumstances. Here lies the justification for having elected bodies to supervise the administration of local services – health, education, the police, and so on – and to take responsibility for local government in general.

Elections and the judiciary

Should the judiciary be elected? At first sight, consistency would seem to require that, just as the legislature and chief executive are popularly elected, so should the judiciary be. However, since the judiciary serves a legal rather than a political function, whose virtue lies in consistency and impartiality rather than popularity, the tenure of office should be immune from popular disapproval or the danger of becoming too closely identified with a particular section of the community. It is the task of parliament to ensure that legislation, levels of sentencing, and so on, remain in touch with public opinion, not that of the judiciary itself. At the same time, the pattern of recruitment to the judiciary is a matter of legitimate democratic concern, especially where it works to disadvantage substantial sections of society, such as women or members of ethnic or other minorities.

32. Should there be more than one elected chamber of parliament?

The functions of a parliament or legislature are to scrutinize and approve legislation, taxation and public expenditure; to provide oversight of the government; to ratify treaties and to oversee avenues of complaint and redress for the public in the event of maladministration. The argument for having a second or upper chamber of parliament, elected on a different basis from the first or lower chamber, rests on the desirability of ensuring the fullest consideration and the widest support in carrying out these functions. It is particularly important in a federal system, where the second chamber represents the interests of the member states rather than of the territory considered as a whole. A second chamber can also serve to make parliament as a whole more inclusive, by ensuring representation for different social groups of the population, and for those citizens living outside the country.

Different elections

Methods of election will normally differ between the two chambers, with the upper one being elected indirectly, or on the basis of different constituencies, or over a different timescale so that, say, only a proportion of members comes up for election at any one time. In a parliamentary system, the simultaneous direct election of the lower chamber by the country as a whole makes it the chief source of popular legitimacy for government, and gives it the priority in legislation; at most the upper chamber will have a limited delaying or veto power. This priority of the lower chamber is especially marked in countries where the upper chamber is wholly or largely appointed without competitive election.

33. How frequently should elections take place?

The demand of radical democrats in nineteenth-century Europe was for annual elections to parliament, in order to keep effective control over representatives. However, the business of modern government and parliament requires a longer time-span than one year for the effective management of the economy, and for the consequences of policies to work through. A four-year cycle is now usually accepted as a reasonable compromise between a government's need for continuity, on the one hand, and the requirements of responsiveness and accountability, on the other. However, variations around this norm are to be found, as in the United States of America (USA), where members of the House of Representatives are elected for two years, whereas members of the Senate serve for a six-year term.

Timing of elections

Whatever the precise duration of the elected offices, however, it is important that the timing of an election does not rest with the government in power. As will be discussed below (see question 43), it is a cardinal principle of 'free and fair' elections that the electoral process should not be controlled by, or give an unfair advantage to, the party or parties in office. This requirement should extend to the timing, as well as the conduct, of elections.

34. Should anyone be denied the right to vote?

The usual exclusions operating in most democracies are for children, convicted criminals and foreign residents. This is a very 'mixed bag', and there are different rationales for each category. The exclusion of children below a certain age is justified by both common sense and developmental psychology. Below a certain age, most children do not have sufficient experience or sufficient sense of the long-term consequences of their choices to be treated non-paternalistically. In most societies, there is a 'clustering' of rights which children attain together and which define adulthood: the right to marry, to own property, to initiate legal proceedings in one's own person, and to vote. These usually coincide around the age of eighteen, with the latest age for leaving secondary school and with the obligation for military service.

Determinate age limit

Any fixed age, however, is bound to be somewhat arbitrary. There is evidence that children nowadays mature earlier than in the past. Some rights, e.g. to earn wages in full-time employment, they attain before eighteen. And there is regrettable truth in the argument that some children need protection *from* the adults who are supposedly responsible for them, and that this requires them to be given a say in their lives much earlier. In any case, maturing is a continuous process, and preparation for democratic citizenship should involve some participation in collective decision-making in family and school from the earliest age possible. However, none of these considerations is sufficiently compelling to merit lowering the voting age in public elections significantly below eighteen, or to undermine the symbolic importance of having a particular moment when everyone is recognized by society as attaining the status and rights of adulthood together.

Criminals and the vote

The argument for debarring criminals serving prison sentences from the vote is that those found guilty of serious offences against the law have forfeited the right to any say in framing it. On the other side, though, it can be argued that the loss of freedom should not entail the loss of all other rights of citizenship; and that prisoners particularly require access to elected representatives to help protect them against illegal or inhumane treatment and conditions. In a judgement of the European Court of Human Rights in 2005 (6.10.05), the Court ruled that denying convicted prisoners the vote was a breach of their human rights. The denial of the vote, said the judges, 'runs counter to the rehabilitation of the offender as a law-abiding member of the community'.

Resident aliens

Finally, and most contentiously, is the exclusion of resident aliens. Here the right to vote involves the larger question of the qualifications for access to citizenship. If we acknowledge that democracy emerged from the eighteenth-century challenge to the dynastic principle of birth or inheritance as the exclusive basis for political rights, then we should not with consistency make it the sole criterion of citizenship to the exclusion of legally settled residence in a country. What period of time would count as being 'settled' may be a matter of dispute, but a period of no more than five years would be a reasonable requirement for application for citizenship for those who so choose.

35. What should be the procedures for voter registration?

Voter registration sounds like a technical matter, but in practice the procedures adopted have a considerable significance for the right to vote. The point of having a register of electors compiled prior to an election taking place is simple: voters have to be identified in person and their act of voting recorded so that no one votes twice, impersonates another voter, or otherwise votes without being entitled to do so.

The importance of compulsory registration

There are various ways in which the procedures for registration may discourage citizens from having their entitlement registered, or from exercising it in practice. Registration may be voluntary, and may depend upon the unpaid efforts of party volunteers. It may take place so long before an election that it is already well out of date when the election is called. Or the register may be used for other state purposes, such as a record of taxation, marital or occupational status, which citizens should properly be required to declare separately. The procedure which accords with best democratic practice is that registration should be compulsory, that the compilation of the register should be carried out by paid officials trained for the purpose, and as near as practicable to an election, and that it be kept physically and organizationally separate from other state records.

36. Does voter turnout matter?

In many countries the proportion of registered electors who actually vote is in long-term decline, though there can be considerable variation between different elections in any one country. Where the result of an election seems a foregone conclusion, or not much seems to hang on the outcome, turnouts can drop sharply. But the long-term decline in many countries is also a worrying indication that all may not be well with the democratic process. In opinion surveys, many voters express considerable disaffection with politicians as a whole, seeing them as self-serving and out of touch with the concerns of people like themselves. There is also the recognition that differences of principle between political parties have become increasingly blurred, as the scope for policy initiatives on the part of governments has been substantially reduced by the pressures of globalization and the requirements of international institutions.

Measures to improve turnout

One way of improving voter turnout is to make it easier to actually cast one's vote. Various experiments have been undertaken recently in established democracies to enable people to vote from home, rather than having to make a trip to the polling station. Thus,

arrangements for postal voting can be extended to include not just those who are sick, disabled or away from home, but anyone who wishes to vote this way. More ambitiously, voting by electronic means from home or the workplace is being considered in some countries. After all, internet banking is now becoming standard, and people are becoming used to voting by phone to determine the outcome of television shows. Could this not be extended to elections, and might this not be a way of interesting young people in politics? The problem with voting from home, however, is that it enormously increases the opportunities for fraud and impersonation; and it can make voters vulnerable to improper pressure within the family. In any case, purely technical fixes cannot address the underlying problems of voter alienation, nor absolve politicians from the responsibility to re-engage more effectively with the needs and concerns of their voters.

Compulsory voting

The argument for making voting compulsory (as, for example, in Australia) is that helping to choose a government and to elect representatives is a civic duty as well as a right, and one which past generations have struggled to achieve. The act of abstention should be positively recorded on the ballot paper, rather than simply being expressed by non-attendance, along with the apathetic, the absent and the deceased. Against this it can be argued that there is something contradictory about making a 'free election' compulsory, or requiring people to exercise their 'rights'; and that levels of voter abstention, and their incidence as between different groups of the population, constitute an important signal or early warning sign of inadequacies in the democratic process, which should not be covered up.

37. Who can stand for election to public office?

In principle anyone entitled to vote can also stand for election, though some countries require a higher age threshold for candidates than for voters. Other than that, no particular requirements are necessary. We elect representatives not for any special expertise they may possess, but because we trust them to do a conscientious job in defending constituents' interests, in scrutinizing the work and the proposals of government, and in promoting the programme on which they have been elected. Any reasonably intelligent, conscientious, organized and articulate person is capable of doing this, whatever walk of life they come from. Once elected, they will have access to the time and the resources necessary to do the job effectively. Over time they will also gain experience; but it is a necessary condition of electoral accountability that the job is not one that can be guaranteed for life.

Individual competition

Although many people, therefore, could do the job of a representative, very few actually become one. The route to doing so is typically lengthy and arduous. In most cases a person will need to be a member of an established political party and have worked for it for a number of years, often with experience of elected office at local or sub-national level. They will then need to convince a party selection board or committee of their suitability, in competition with others, and will probably have to stand unsuccessfully in one or two elections before they achieve a winnable seat or position on the party list. Even then, it might turn out to be a bad year for the party! So it requires a lot of determination as well as luck. Only those with a very strong interest in public affairs, and a readiness to work unsocial hours, will last the course.

Conditions for nomination

A different question concerns the procedures for nomination or registering a candidacy. Most electoral systems seek to deter frivolous candidates by requiring a minimum number of supporting signatures from registered electors in the relevant constituency, and/ or by requiring a monetary deposit, to be forfeited if a minimum number of votes is not obtained. The danger of both practices is that they may deter serious as well as frivolous candidates, especially where they represent new parties or political forces. In some countries only candidates representing previously registered parties may stand. Again, this is designed to deter the frivolous, but it may also serve as a means of political control over parties and candidates, and so limit the legitimate expression of electoral opinion.

Primary elections

In the USA, candidates for each party are chosen by a primary election restricted to the registered voters of the relevant party. Although this practice gives voters a say in who stands for office as well as who is elected to it, it enormously increases the cost of elections, and creates a bias in favour of those who are personally rich or who have wealthy backers. In view of this drawback, it is more usual to have candidates chosen by ballot of all party *members* in the relevant district or constituency, though even this degree of democracy in candidate selection is by no means universal.

38. Why are men and women not equally represented in public office?

The proportion of representatives who are women in Western democracies is very low compared with the proportion of women in the electorate. The average for long-established democracies is around 18 per cent, ranging from a mean of around 40 per cent for the Nordic countries to around 10 per cent for most of the rest, with a low of 6 per cent for the lowest. The reasons for this situation are partly historical, partly domestic, and partly political. For most of human history women have been considered naturally unsuited to political activity, and have been formally or informally excluded from it, thus reinforcing the belief in their unsuitability. The legacy of these past beliefs, reinforced by the unequal domestic division of labour, whereby women continue to take the major responsibility

for child rearing and servicing the home, handicaps women in the pursuit of political office. Politics is an enormously time-consuming activity; the hours worked by government and parliament are often highly unsocial; and the activity itself, which puts a premium on competition, party rivalry and personal aggrandisement, is one that women tend to find more uncongenial than men.

Why equality matters

Does this matter? From the standpoint of political equality it matters if any section of society is markedly privileged in its access to public office, whether elected or non-elected. There is also good reason to suppose that issues affecting women are not taken so seriously by men, or given sufficient priority in the competition for public funding. Although women do not by any means all have the same views and interests, there is something offensive to many women about a largely male parliament deciding legislation on contraception, abortion, rape and so on. In any case, society as a whole is the poorer if the distinctive attributes and characteristics developed by women are not given due scope in public life.

Changing the balance

What can be done? Overcoming a historical legacy of political inequality requires relevant action at a number of levels: changing attitudes through schools and public education; improving childcare facilities; reviewing the schedules and facilities of parliament; and much more. Political parties have a special responsibility to take the lead in encouraging women members, and to put them forward as candidates for election, whether through the operation of quotas, reserved places or other means, as has been done successfully in the Nordic countries. These and other affirmative action measures can be justified by reference to Article 4.1 of the UN Convention on the Elimination of All Forms of Discrimination against Women: 'Adoption by States Parties of temporary special measures aimed at accelerating *de facto* equality between men and women shall not be considered discrimination'.

Women in recently established parliaments

Apart from the Nordic countries, some of the more recently established or restored parliaments have relatively high proportions of women members (for example Rwanda, 49 per cent; Argentina, 31 per cent; South Africa, 30 per cent; Viet Nam, 27 per cent; Bulgaria, 26 per cent; Uganda, 25 per cent (source: Inter-Parliamentary Union). One reason for it being easier for women to get elected to new parliaments is that there are no sitting male parliamentarians to resist being displaced. The clearest demonstration of this effect can be seen by comparing the proportion of women in the new Scottish Parliament and Welsh Assembly (40 per cent and 50 per cent respectively) with the proportion of women from those two nations elected to the UK Parliament at Westminster (around 15 per cent).

39. In what sense do parliamentary representatives 'represent' the electorate?

There are two basic meanings of political representation. The first is the *agency* concept, whereby the representative is seen as 'authorized by', 'standing for', 'acting on behalf of' his or her constituents. In some respects the representative acts on behalf of *all* his or her constituents or electorate: for example, in the promotion of local interests, in the articulation of local opinion, or in pursuing remedies for individual grievances. In other respects the representative only represents those who voted for him or her: by carrying through the programme and policies which constituted the electoral platform, and which were rejected by some constituents as much as they were approved by others. The idea that parliamentary representatives speak and act for all their constituents in all respects is a fiction, which is simply incompatible with their responsibility to act consistently with the programme on which they were elected, and to be accountable for its effective fulfilment.

Microcosmic representation

The second concept of political representation is a *microcosmic* one, and concerns the representative assembly as a whole, rather than individual representatives. A legislative assembly can be said to be 'representative' to the extent that it reflects the character of the electorate at large in some relevant respect: its social composition, its geographical distribution, or its overall votes for the respective parties. Which of these respects is most important? All matter, but in a system where the electoral choice is between national parties offering competing programmes of legislation, the requirement that the assembly's composition reflect the national vote for the respective parties can be argued to be the most important. It is most fully met in proportional electoral systems (see question 40).

Two democratic principles

These two concepts of representation, the agential and the microcosmic, can be seen to embody the two basic principles of democracy already outlined (see question 1). The principle of popular sovereignty – that all political authority stems from the people, and that parliament and government should be subject to popular control – is encapsulated in the idea of the representative as *agent* of the electorate: authorized by, acting for, accountable to, and removable by, them. The second, *microcosmic*, conception of representation embraces the principle of political equality: each vote should have the same weight or value, regardless of where a person happens to live or which party they vote for. To the extent that this principle is met, the assembly will be microcosmically representative of the electorate, and reflect its geographical distribution and the distribution of the popular vote between the different parties.

40. What are the differences between different electoral systems?

There are numerous electoral systems in use throughout the world, and only the five main types will be outlined here. The respective merits of each will be considered in the answer to the next question; here they are simply described.

The plurality system

The plurality or 'first past the post' system is used for legislative elections in the USA, most of Latin America, and also in the United Kingdom (UK) and many of its former colonies. Under this system the country is divided into single-member constituencies of roughly equal size. Voters may vote for only one candidate on the ballot paper, and the candidate who wins the most votes is elected, whether or not he or she wins a majority of the votes cast. This is what the term 'plurality' means.

The alternative vote

The alternative vote is used for the Australian lower house. Here the constituency system is as above, but the voter puts a preference ordering against the candidates. If no candidate wins an outright majority of first preferences, the candidate with the fewest votes is eliminated, and his or her ballot papers are reallocated according to second preferences. This process continues until one candidate achieves a majority of the votes. A majority result can also be achieved by holding a second ballot in which only the top two candidates from the first round of voting go into the second (as in France).

The single transferable vote

The single transferable vote is used in Ireland, Malta and the Australian Senate. Here the constituencies return a number of members, usually between 3 and 7 according to population density. Voters have as many votes as there are representatives to be elected, which they list in order of preference. To be elected, a candidate has to achieve a certain 'quota' or proportion of the votes cast. Those who fail to achieve the quota on the first preferences may do so on second and later-order preferences, according to a given formula for the redistribution of these preferences.

The party list

The party list system is used in most countries of Western and Eastern Europe, and some countries of Africa and Asia. Here the parties draw up regional or national lists of candidates in a ranking order, and the voter casts one vote for his or her favoured party. Candidates are then elected in proportion to the total votes cast for the respective parties. A party may be required to achieve a minimum proportion of the vote to win any representation.

The mixed member system

The mixed member, or additional member, system, though not widespread, is becoming increasingly popular in many regions of the world as a compromise between the plurality and party list systems. Under this system a proportion of representatives (at least 50 per cent) is elected in single-member constituencies, as in the first two systems above. The remaining representatives are elected under a party list system, either regional or national, in such a manner as to make the result more 'proportional' to the distribution of the overall party vote. Electors have two votes, one for a candidate and one for a party. Again there may be a minimum threshold which parties have to attain in order to qualify for representation.

41. What are the advantages and disadvantages of these systems?

The precise merits of different electoral systems cannot adequately be assessed separately from the character and distribution of a country's population, and the pattern of electoral support for its different parties. For example, if a country lacks established political parties altogether, then a 'proportional' electoral system makes no sense, since it is the distribution of the popular vote between the respective parties that constitutes the focus of proportionality. The following assessment should therefore be read as identifying the general tendencies of different systems, rather than their inevitable effects.

Simplicity
The *plurality* system ('first past the post') has the merit of simplicity. It is more likely than other systems to produce single-party majorities in parliament, and hence single-party government, since it exaggerates the electoral support for the largest party. It is also able to register small shifts in electoral opinion to bring about a change of government, though this effect will depend upon the number of 'marginal' constituencies. The disadvantage of the system is that it can produce extremely disproportionate outcomes, depending on how the national vote is distributed between the parties and between the different constituencies. Thus, for example, if every constituency mirrored exactly a national distribution of support between four parties in the ratio 40, 30, 20, 10, then one party could theoretically win all the seats in parliament, and 60 per cent of

the voters would not be represented. Of course this never happens. But the system favours parties whose vote is concentrated in certain areas rather than thinly spread, and puts a considerable premium on how constituency boundaries are drawn. It also encourages voters to vote tactically, not necessarily voting for their first choice, but with arbitrary results, since they cannot know with certainty how other voters will behave.

Majority support

The *alternative vote* has the advantage over the plurality system in that it will almost certainly require a candidate to win a majority of votes in a constituency in order to be elected, whereas the plurality system does not. Winning such a majority could be seen as a minimum requirement for legitimately representing a constituency. Its overall effect is also likely to be more proportional than the plurality system. However, it could still prevent third and fourth parties with a substantial but evenly spread support from being represented in parliament.

Voter choice

The *single transferable vote* enables smaller parties to achieve representation, though how proportionately will depend upon the size of the constituencies (the larger, the more proportionate). Supporters of a given party are also able to express preferences between its candidates. However, the large size of constituencies tends to break the link between representatives and their electorate that is found in single-member constituencies; and the mechanism for distributing lower preference votes between the candidates is extraordinarily complicated.

Proportionality

The *party list* system can claim to give the most nearly equal weight to each vote, and thus to produce the most proportionate distribution of seats to the votes cast for the respective parties. Its disadvantages are that there is no direct accountability of representatives to a given body of constituents, and that the electorate (and even party members) may have no influence over the respective ordering of a party's candidates on the list. Representatives may thus be beholden more to the central party organization than to the electorate. The list system does, however, give parties both the opportunity and the incentive to produce a 'balanced' slate of candidates, as between different party tendencies and between different social groups.

Differential representation

The *mixed member* system can produce more or less proportionate outcomes according to what proportion of representatives are elected in single-member constituencies. It could thus be designed to produce single-party government when there was a strong surge of support for one party, while requiring coalition government in the event of a more even distribution of the popular vote. Besides the disadvantages of the list system, however, it also requires two different kinds of representative, those with constituencies and those without them. Supporters of the system argue that these disadvantages could be overcome by constructing the party lists from the best losers in the constituency contests, and by allocating these members to given constituencies for constituency responsibilities.

42. Is coalition government undemocratic?

Supporters of proportional representation argue that the plurality and alternative vote systems are undemocratic because they treat citizens' votes unequally, allowing much greater weight to some than to others. They thus infringe the basic democratic principle of political equality. In doing so they can allow governments to be elected which only have the support of a minority of the electorate, sometimes a quite small minority. On the other side, critics of proportional representation contend that, because it is rare for any single party ever to win a majority of the popular vote, under such a system coalition government will always be required. And coalitions take the determination of governments out of the hands of the electors and give them to the party bosses, thus reducing the degree of popular control and accountability. They may also give a disproportionate amount of power to minority parties, especially if they occupy a 'hinge' position in the centre between larger parties of Left and Right. To this it may be objected in turn that all parties will have to account to their electorates for the coalition decisions they make; and that centre parties cannot simply ignore the relative shift in votes between parties of the Left and Right from one election to the next.

Particular circumstances

Once more, it is difficult to decide upon the balance of the argument in abstraction from a particular country and its circumstances. The recent history of the UK has exposed the inadequacies of the simple plurality system as clearly as the recent history of Italy has shown the deficiencies of a purely proportional one. It may well be that a system which combines the strengths of constituency representation with some counterbalancing element of proportionality is likely to prove most serviceable, though the precise relation between the two must depend upon the context of party development and the wider constitutional arrangements. For example, in societies politically divided along ethnic or religious lines, an electoral system which encourages inclusive, power-sharing government is usually preferable to the majoritarian, 'winner-take-all' effects of the plurality system.

43. How can the fairness of the election process be guaranteed?

There are three main sources for threats to the fairness of the election process. The first comes from the advantage that being in government gives to the ruling party or parties. This can never be entirely eliminated, but it can be minimized by a number of measures. Most important is that the whole election process – from the drawing of electoral boundaries, through the registration of voters and the conduct of the campaign, to the election itself and the counting of votes – should be supervised by an independent electoral commission, whose membership should require the approval of all political parties. Among its duties should be to regulate the access of parties to the publicly owned media during the campaign, if there is not an independent broadcasting commission to do so. Also of importance is that the organization of parties should be legally separated from the organization of government, and that ministers be required to surrender all official duties and privileges for the duration of the election campaign, other than those necessary to the guarantee of law and order in its conduct.

Electoral malpractice

A second threat to the fairness of the election process stems from all kinds of malpractice by candidates, party members and their supporters. Examples of malpractice include: bribing electors, preventing them from registering to vote, threatening them, impersonating voters, disrupting meetings of opposing candidates, seizing ballot boxes, stuffing them with your own votes, rigging the count, and many more. These can only be avoided if adequate personnel, both police and election officials, are assigned to ensure the physical security of candidates and voters, and to protect the integrity of the election process. Of particular importance is the calibre of election officials, whose appointment and training should be the responsibility of the national electoral commission. The presence of experienced international observers may be of particular assistance; indeed there is a good argument for making their presence a standard feature of national elections in all democratic countries, to act as both an external guarantor of fair conduct and a disseminator of best electoral practice. International standards for 'free and fair' elections and for election monitoring have now become codified, and are widely accepted.

Influence of wealth

A final major threat to the fairness of the election process arises from the advantage that the possession of personal wealth or access to wealthy backers can give to individual candidates or parties (see also question 56). The simplest way to offset this is to set strict limits to the amounts of money that can be spent by and on behalf of candidates and parties, both nationally and locally; and to provide them all with free access to the publicly owned media, according to guidelines approved by the electoral commission or its equivalent.

Opinion polls

Of lesser threats to electoral fairness, the operation of opinion polls is under discussion in a number of countries. Some already have legislation banning the publication of opinion polls during the last week of the election or over the election period as a whole. The assumption is that such polls can affect the outcome of the election itself, through either a 'bandwagon' or 'counter-bandwagon' effect, and that they encourage an unhealthy concentration on the anticipated result and the exclusion of the issues which should determine it. However, most experts are sceptical about the influence of opinion polls on voting, and are doubtful about the practicability of suppressing them when people increasingly have access to the international media.

44. Should political parties be publicly funded?

The main arguments in favour of public financing of political parties are that they play a vital political role in a democratic system, which should be recognized by financial support; and that public funding would diminish the influence of powerful vested interests on the political process, creating a more level playing field between the parties. The ever-increasing cost of the electoral 'arms race' in all countries has two damaging consequences. One is that wealthy individual and corporate sponsors of party campaigns come to exercise more influence over the policy and legislative process than the voters do. The other is that only the personally wealthy can afford the costs involved in standing for public office. Public funding could offset these effects, without necessarily undermining the incentive parties have to recruit members or win votes. Thus, parties could be financed in proportion to the votes cast for them in each national election or to their audited membership. And public finance could be denied to a party that campaigned to deprive any group of its civil and political rights, or that was convicted of electoral malpractice.

Party autonomy
The chief argument against public funding is that political parties can only be an effective vehicle for popular opinion from below to the extent that they maintain their autonomy from the state; and voluntary funding is a necessary condition for such autonomy.

If parties cannot maintain sufficient support for their activities from voluntary contributions, then they do not deserve to be considered seriously for public office. At the same time, the undue influence of special interests can be curtailed if all donations to a party above a certain amount must be publicly declared; and if all institutional supporters are required to obtain the explicit agreement of their members, shareholders, etc., for any donations they make.

Limited public support

Most established democracies expect their parties to be financed from voluntary sources. However, this need not exclude limited public finance for carefully delimited activities, such as the training of party cadres, or free access to the publicly owned media at election time. Such financial support may be particularly necessary in a period of transition to democracy, when parties may have to be started from scratch, and there is little recent experience of electoral competition.

45. Should elected representatives be allowed to change their party allegiance between elections?

This is a controversial issue. By standing for election under a given party label, candidates are in effect committing themselves to the support of that party for the term of office. If that were not so, the use of the vote to choose between different programmes and political tendencies would be rendered meaningless. In addition, 'floor-crossing', 'party-hopping' or 'political nomadism', as it is variously called, may be quite self-serving, for example in pursuit of governmental office; and it can bring considerable instability to parliament as well as frustrating the clear will of the electors. For these reasons a number of parliaments have introduced anti-defection provisions, requiring a member who has joined another party in mid-term (or even voted against their party) to surrender his or her seat, or to stand for a by-election if it is a constituency-based system. The problem with such provisions is that they infringe an accepted principle that parliamentarians should be free to speak and act as they see fit in the interests of their constituents; and that they should only forfeit their seat following conviction for a criminal offence, and by a decision of the legislature as a whole.

46. Do voters have any power between elections?

It is mistaken to imagine that, because the only political act voters may undertake is to cast their vote once every four years or so, they are powerless in between. The *prospect* of having to face the electorate in the future constitutes an important discipline on governing parties, and compels them to consult public opinion on a continuous basis. In other words, elections cast a long shadow in front of them. This is particularly evident in a constituency-based electoral system, where defeat for a governing party in a by-election may lead to dramatic shifts in policy and even of leadership. In addition, there are a variety of civil society channels for voters to exert influence over government on specific issues in between elections, such as membership of pressure groups and voluntary associations, contributing to public campaigns, contacting representatives and members of government, taking part in demonstrations, and so on. The use of the internet now makes it much easier to follow the proceedings of government and parliament, to take part in pre-legislative consultations, and to interrogate individual representatives on key votes and policies (see question 50).

47. When should referenda be held in a democracy?

Most democracies require referenda to be held, sometimes by qualified majority, in the event of proposed changes to the constitution or legislation that has substantial constitutional implications. The reason is that a constitution belongs to the people as a whole, not to members of parliament or the government of the day; and it should therefore be subject to direct popular approval.

Referenda on other legislation

In some countries referenda are permitted on substantive issues of policy and legislation as well, usually only after the collection of a prescribed number of signatures supporting the proposal. Such referenda may take the form of a retrospective veto on existing legislation. Or they may allow for a positive citizens' initiative proposing new legislation, which may then be either advisory on the legislature or mandatory. Those in favour of the use of referenda argue that they constitute a key democratic device, which allows the population a direct say on important issues that may otherwise be simply ignored or lost in the generality of a party's election manifesto. Against this, it can be contended that, since so many issues of political decision are interconnected (e.g. taxation and public spending), it is arbitrary to take one issue out of context, and require it to be decided by a group of people different from those who have the responsibility for all the other decisions.

No right answer

This is one of those issues where there is no right or wrong answer, and different democracies will adopt different practices according to their own political tradition. However, it is worth noting that the practice of allowing legislative referenda and citizens' initiatives, which used to be confined to Italy, Switzerland and certain states in the USA, is now becoming more widespread, including such countries as Costa Rica, the former Yugoslav Republic of Macedonia, Portugal and Slovenia; many others are actively considering it. One reason is that a popular device of this kind is now being seen as a means to help reduce the gap between legislatures and their electorate. The requirement that such initiatives should not infringe constitutionally guaranteed rights, say of minorities or other sections of society, provides a necessary safeguard against their abuse.

4. Open and Accountable Government

48. In what ways is open government important to democracy?

Open government is essential to democracy because public officials cannot be held accountable, nor citizens make an informed electoral choice, unless there is accurate information available about the activity of government and the consequences of its policies. Access to such information should be seen as a right of citizens and of the media on their behalf, rather than as a favour of governments, since it is the electorate which pays the bills to keep government going; it should therefore know what it is getting for its money, and what is being done in its name. Although providing such access is often criticized as itself a drain on public resources, it has its own contribution to make to government efficiency, in helping to expose waste, inhibit corruption and identify policy errors before they become chronic. It is also an important element in the protection of civil liberties that individuals should have access to personal files held on them by government and its agencies.

Aspects of open government

What exactly does open government involve? Open government can be seen as having four main strands. First is the provision by government itself of factual information about its policies: the evidence on which they are based, their consequences in practice, their cost, the rules governing their operation, and so on. Second is the access of individuals and the press to government documents, both directly and indirectly through parliament; this will include the accessibility of personal files to the individuals concerned. Third is the openness of meetings to the public and the press; this can typically range from parliament and its committees, to the proceedings of publicly funded agencies and the meetings of local government. Fourth is the systematic consultation by government of relevant interests in the formulation and implementation of policy, and the publication of the information and advice so received.

Legitimate exceptions

Are there any exceptions to the principle of open government? The categories of information which are usually justified as legitimately confidential in a democracy include: the deliberations of cabinet; political advice given to ministers by civil servants; information whose publication would damage national defence, the security of the democratic system or the physical safety of individuals; trade secrets of private firms; and personal files, except to the individuals concerned.

49. How can open government be secured?

In the pre-twentieth-century era of limited government, it was thought sufficient for ensuring open government to guarantee the freedom of the press. Nowadays, with much more complex and far-reaching state activity, even the most stringent guarantees of press freedom, including provision for protecting the confidentiality of journalists' sources, are insufficient on their own. The characteristic tendency of governments and their bureaucracies is to cloak their activities in secrecy, so as to protect error or misdemeanour, to avoid embarrassment, or simply to preserve their conviction that they know best. This tendency can nowadays only be effectively counteracted by legislation requiring open government, or 'freedom of information'.

Freedom of information

Model legislation for freedom of information, setting standards of 'best practice', is provided by the USA and Sweden. This covers all the main areas mentioned earlier (see question 48): the duty of government disclosure; the right of public access to documents; the openness of meetings of public agencies; also the protection of 'whistle-blowers', who leak evidence of malpractice or illegality

within the government service. Such legislation should be seen as additional, and complementary, to measures guaranteeing the right of parliament or legislature to scrutinize the executive. An important feature of such legislation is that the interpretation of the exceptions to disclosure (e.g. those necessary to national security, to protect privacy) is vested with the courts rather than the government itself.

Public relations and 'spin'

Two further issues deserve mention. First, modern governments are characterized by the enormous budgets devoted to 'public relations'. This embraces not only factual information about government policy, but its timing and presentation so as to maximize favourable impact, the practice of selective leaking, and all the other devices in the public relations armoury used to massage public opinion, which go under the name of 'spin'. These practices make the guarantee of independent access to, and testing of, government information especially crucial. Of particular importance here is the existence of a public statistical service, independent of government, on which government, parliament and the public can draw equally.

Public consultation

Finally, open government as a concept is much broader than simply freedom of information. It includes the accessibility of ministers to justify and debate their policies in public, and the degree to which government is required to consult the public in its formulation and implementation of policy. This latter involves legislation covering such issues as: requisite timescales and procedures for consultation; the publication of evidence from interested parties; the assessment of environmental impact; and so forth. 'Openness' thus comprises the readiness to listen as well as to make available access to accurate information.

50. What is electronic democracy?

Electronic democracy (e-democracy) is based on a market–driven technology which some have argued is entirely neutral in application, since it can be used as readily by governments for increased surveillance or control as by citizens for their own communication. Yet a plausible case can be made for concluding that the technology has an inherent bias towards empowering the citizen, in the following ways:

- It enables information of all kinds about government and parliament to be directly accessible to citizens in their own homes.
- It radically increases the speed of communication, while cutting its cost to virtually nothing, so facilitating contact and organization between citizens, and between them and their representatives
- It is an interactive medium, which facilitates new forms of discussion and debate that transcend all spatial limitations.
- It is beyond the control of governments, whether control of its use or its development, and it makes national borders and censorships largely irrelevant.

Some disadvantages

The advantages already listed can benefit uncivil groups (criminal gangs, paedophiles, racist organizations) as well as civil or democratic ones, but this is a small price to pay for the wider democratic potential of the technology. Much more serious from a democratic point of view is that all its advantages are dependent on the ability to access it, and this ability is very unequally distributed between different groups of citizens. The greater the empowering capacity of the technology, the greater the deprivation for those who cannot access or use it. These inequalities are also very marked between the world's regions, as proportions of the population with access to the internet in the year 2005 demonstrate: North America, 67.4 per cent; Oceania, 48.6 per cent; Europe, 35.5 per cent; Latin America/Caribbean, 10.3 per cent; Asia, 8.4 per cent; Middle East, 7.5 per cent; Africa,1.5 per cent (source: Internet World Statistics).

51. What is meant by accountable government?

The concept of accountable government has three main dimensions.

Legal accountability

First is *legal accountability*: the accountability of all public officials, elected and non-elected, to the courts for the legality of their actions. Here lies the basic meaning of the 'rule of law', that those who make and execute law and policy must themselves act under and within the law and the constitution, on the basis of powers which are legally defined and circumscribed.

Political accountability

The second aspect is *political accountability*: the accountability of the government or executive to parliament and public for the justifiability of its policies, their prioritization and their manner of execution. Where the first, legal, type of accountability has a relatively simple structure, as between public officials and the courts, political accountability is more complex. Non-elected agencies of government at national level (the civil service, armed forces, police, security services) are typically accountable to the elected head of the executive through ministers appointed by him or her. The chief executive and ministers are accountable in turn both to the public directly via the electoral process, and to parliament or legislature acting as agents of the public. Members of the legislature are then accountable to their own electorate.

Financial accountability

Third is the narrower concept of *financial accountability*: the accountability of government for spending the proceeds of taxation only on those purposes approved by the legislature, and in the most cost-effective manner. Here the route of accountability follows closely that of political accountability, with the important addition of an auditor general's office, which is accountable to parliament but acts independently of it in its professional scrutiny of the detail of government expenditure.

Accountability and popular control

These different accountability routes are traced in diagrammatic form in Figure 2. Whereas each of them contributes to the democratic

Figure 2. Accountability Routes

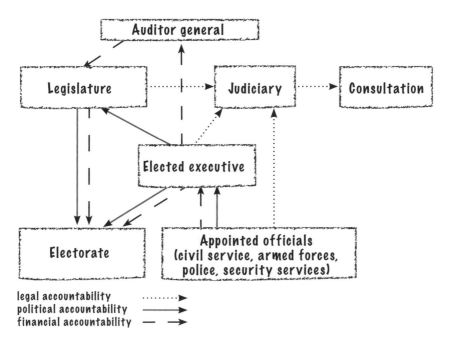

legal accountability   ·········▶
political accountability   ─────▶
financial accountability   ── ─▶

principle of popular control over government, it will be seen that both financial and legal accountability are best secured through professional bodies which operate with a certain degree of immunity from direct public or political influence, and which are accountable to their own professional codes of practice. Ultimately, however, it is political accountability that is supreme, since the legislation which the courts enforce and the expenditure which the auditor-general scrutinizes are themselves dependent upon the authorization of a popularly elected parliament, acting under the constitution. All these can be regarded as forms of what is called 'lateral' accountability, in contrast to the 'vertical' accountability exercised by the electorate itself.

52. Why is the separation of powers important?

In democracies, government is divided into three branches: the executive (sometimes also simply called 'the government'), which is responsible for the formulation and execution of policy; the legislature (also called parliament, representative or national assembly), which is responsible for the approval of legislation and taxation and the scrutiny of the executive; the judiciary (or the courts), which is responsible for securing the observance of the law, by determining whether it has been infringed and sentencing those found guilty of its infringement. This separation of the three branches has proved essential for securing the different forms of accountability mentioned above (see question 51). Thus, if the courts are not independent of both legislature and executive, they cannot act without fear or favour in ensuring that public officials operate within the law. Similarly, if parliament does not have independent powers to approve legislation and taxation, and to scrutinize the executive, the political and financial accountability of government to the electorate will be seriously impaired.

Different systems

Although the separation of powers between executive and legislature is a common feature of democratic government, it is treated differently in different political systems. In a presidential system, where the chief executive is elected separately from the legislature and has no place in it, the separation between the two is most sharply defined. In a prime-ministerial system, on the other hand, where the chief executive is chosen as the party leader who can command a parliamentary majority, he or she has a foot in both camps as it were: acting as head of the executive branch and as leader of the majority in parliament.

Presidentialism

Each system has its respective advantages and disadvantages. The advantage of the presidential system lies typically in the much greater independence of the legislature in its ability to control the executive, although this will also vary according to the degree of organization of political parties, and the balance of party control between the two branches. The corresponding disadvantage lies in what has come to be called 'gridlocked' government: the inability of the executive to secure the necessary legislation and taxation to carry out the policies on which it was directly elected. In extreme circumstances, this separation may result in a struggle for power between the two branches, in which the president may be tempted to use his or her directly elected authority, together with the control of the military, in a plebiscitary coup against the legislature.

Parliament and executive

The advantage of the prime-ministerial system lies in its greater ability to coordinate executive policy with the necessary legislation and taxation; and in the much greater unlikelihood of an executive coup against parliament (a feature that may be particularly relevant to a democratic system only recently established). The corresponding disadvantage lies in the ability of the executive to control the parliamentary agenda, and to limit its scrutinizing function, since members of the parliamentary majority usually have a much greater interest in maintaining the credibility of the government (on which their own seats and future promotion prospects depend) than in exposing its defects to public view.

53. What is the rule of law and how can it be guaranteed?

The 'rule of law' embodies the simple principle that all state officials, whether elected or non-elected, should act within the law and the constitution, on the basis of powers that are legally defined and circumscribed (see legal accountability, question 51). The principle can be traced back to the Aristotelian idea that the best government involves the 'rule of laws, not of men'. In its modern form, the principle evolved from the struggle to limit the arbitrary discretion of the monarch and his officials, by requiring legal authorization for all executive action.

Democracy and the rule of law

The rule of law can be readily seen as a cornerstone of both individual freedom and democracy. Without it there can be no protection of individual rights against the executive. And in so far as the *source* of law is a democratic constitution and an elected legislature, democracy requires that the executive observe it. Attempts to bypass procedural or legal regularity 'in the national interest', or under the pressure of instant popular demand, must therefore be judged undemocratic.

Independence of the judiciary

The rule of law is only effective, however, to the extent that there is an independent judiciary to uphold it. Article 1 of the UN Basic Principles on the Judiciary states that 'the independence of the judiciary shall be guaranteed by the state and enshrined in the constitution or the laws of the country'. This independence is both a collective independence of the institution of the judiciary from interference by the executive, and also a personal independence of individual judges in the performance of their office without fear or favour. Both kinds of independence require more than formal constitutional guarantees; they depend also on the methods by which judges are appointed and on the security of their tenure in office. Appointments should not be in the hands of the government or executive, but should be the responsibility of a judicial committee of parliament or of an independent judicial services committee established under the constitution. Similarly, judges should not be dismissible by the government of the day, but have security of tenure terminable only by special procedure of the appointing body, and for limited causes such as corruption or other gross misdemeanour or dereliction of duty. Similar considerations apply to other branches of the legal profession, whose independence from government is necessary to secure the principle of the rule of law (see also question 58).

54. What contribution does parliament or legislature make to government accountability?

Parliament plays the key role in ensuring the political and financial accountability of the executive. It does this, in the first place, through its powers to approve legislation and taxation, and through the procedures which ensure all measures before it are thoroughly tested and debated before becoming law. Second are the oversight powers of parliament to scrutinize the work of the executive: through questioning ministers, inspecting documents and cross-examining relevant state personnel. These functions are carried out both by parliament sitting as a whole, and through an organized structure of committees.

Parliamentary effectiveness

The effectiveness with which parliament carries out its role of ensuring government accountability depends partly upon the independent-mindedness of individual members. Traditionally, it was thought sufficient to guarantee their independence if they were given immunity from prosecution for anything they said in the chamber, so that they could speak their minds fearlessly. Given the complexity of government business today, however, representatives can only be effectively critical if they have sufficient research and office facilities, and ready access to external expertise. It is also important that they are not so tied to party positions that their critical faculties become blunted. Where members are dependent upon a party hierarchy either for their initial election or for their appointment to specialist committees, they are much less likely to 'step out of line'.

Role of the opposition

However, we should not ignore the important place which the organized party system has in the scrutiny of government. It is the task of an official opposition to not only act as an alternative 'government in waiting', but also coordinate the scrutiny of government through subjecting its work to sustained criticism. Many people find this the least attractive feature of a parliament's work, since it often conveys the impression of 'opposition for opposition's sake', regardless of the merits of any particular government measure. This is indeed true, particularly in the adversarial British system and those parliaments derived from it. Yet, just as modern government is highly organized, so must be the process of scrutinizing it; and this responsibility falls particularly on those parties that do not support the government in power, who should be able to criticize the government fearlessly without their patriotism being brought into question.

55. Should elected representatives be allowed to hold other paid employment?

Although national parliaments may not sit throughout the year, their work is continuous and demanding, and almost all countries regard it as a full-time occupation and pay an appropriate salary accordingly. They differ widely, however, in how far they allow their members to undertake other paid employment, over and above the journalistic and media activity which can be seen as an essential part of a parliamentarian's public function. Those that prohibit other employment argue that parliamentarians should not be treated differently in this regard from all other public sector employees. Those that allow it justify doing so on the ground that outside employment helps keep members in touch with the 'real world'. Where it is allowed, it is now increasingly accepted that all sources of outside income should be declared in a 'register of interests' (see below).

'Money politics'

Nothing has discredited parliaments more as institutions in recent times than the well-founded suspicion that their members are subservient to powerful business and financial interests which have helped finance their electoral campaigns, or paid them 'retainers' to represent their interests in the parliament or legislature. As a result, many parliaments have instituted strict codes of conduct requiring members to not only declare all sources of income and financial and business connections on a register, but to not take part in any public business where a 'conflict of interest' might be involved. Such codes, however, depend for their effectiveness on strict and impartial enforcement. And it must remain a matter of concern that parliamentarians should represent powerful sectional interests and lobbies rather than the mass of their constituents.

Termination of office

A characteristic feature of a representative's position is that it may be terminated abruptly by the electorate, not necessarily for any failing on the individual's part, but because the party's leader and programme are no longer acceptable. Actually this is not all that different from employees in private industry being made suddenly redundant because of market shifts which are none of their fault. Both types of worker should have access to decent severance pay, according to the years worked, to enable them to find alternative employment; and they should enjoy transferable pension rights.

56. How can political corruption be minimized?

Political corruption – the abuse of public office for private gain – can occur at any level of government, and in any political system. It can take many different forms, from parliamentarians legislating in favour of business sectors which have helped finance their election campaigns, to ministers and officials taking bribes for the award of government contracts or trading licences, or public servants expecting personal payment from members of the public for services which they are employed to provide for free. Although in some democracies such payments may be condoned as the expected 'perks of office', they destroy the trust between representatives and their constituents and undermine confidence in the democratic process, to the point where people may not think democracy worth defending. For this reason corruption has to be treated seriously, and efforts made to minimize it, even if it can never be completely eradicated. The international NGO Transparency International, which has branches in most countries, publishes an annual Corruption Perception Index, which scores and ranks countries on a scale of perceived corruption. On this scale, most developing countries score much worse than most developed ones, though the latter score badly in a comparable Bribe Payers Index, which measures the propensity of companies from the top exporting countries to bribe in emerging markets. Corruption is thus a two-sided process.

Remedial measures
Political corruption tends to flourish in the following conditions: where the pay for public office is comparatively low or inadequate, or where, alternatively, it constitutes the only societal avenue to a decent income; where economic opportunities in the private

sector are particularly dependent upon discretionary government decisions; and where the chances of being exposed and punished are low. The above conditions suggest their corresponding antidotes: to pay public officials decently, though not excessively in comparison with other jobs; to subject all government decisions affecting private economic agents to clearly defined rules and procedures; and to combine open government with fearless judicial investigation of suspected illegality, for example by an anti-corruption commission vested with judicial powers.

Public service ethos

The best inoculation against corruption is the development over time of a culture and tradition of disinterested public service, which is not penetrated too far by the market philosophy of self-interest maximization. Besides a Convention against Corruption, the UN has also developed an International Code of Conduct for Public Officials (1997). This requires that all public officials act in the public interest, and do not use their official authority for the improper advancement of their own or their family's personal or financial interest; nor receive any gift or other favour that might influence the impartial exercise of their functions.

57. What role does the civil service play in a democracy?

The full-time non-elected officials of the civil service constitute the permanent administration on which government relies for conducting its day to day business. They provide both the expert advice necessary to the formulation of policy and legislation, and the administrative structure necessary to carrying it out effectively. They are expected to perform these roles conscientiously and impartially, whatever party or parties are in government, and whether they agree personally with the tendency of government policy or not. Although a professional civil service is characteristic of every contemporary system of government, a number of issues arise which are particular to the organization of a civil service in a democracy, such as: how the top civil servants are appointed; to whom civil servants should be accountable; and the pattern of their recruitment.

Political appointments
The first of these issues arises out of a concern expressed within many political parties that, precisely because higher civil servants

are not committed to the policies of the party in power, they may act to obstruct it, or use their monopoly of expertise to provide 'loaded' advice to ministers, who are typically much less expert than their advisers. These concerns are often overstated. It is the responsibility of civil servants to test every policy proposal against objections and practical difficulties, as well as to find ways of carrying it out; and this can often be interpreted as obstructionism. However, it is also true that the civil service constitutes a powerful non-elected influence on policy, and that this influence is capable of being used undemocratically. Established democracies generally use one of two methods to minimize this possibility. One is to make the top administrative post or posts in each ministry subject to political appointment, in principle changing with every change in the elected government. The other is the establishment of a political office in each ministry, staffed by specialists who are also party supporters, and who can provide alternative advice and information to the minister, and have the expertise to provide an independent check on the advice offered by the permanent civil service. Neither method is entirely problem-free, but the advantages probably outweigh the disadvantages.

Civil service accountability

A second issue concerns the accountability of civil servants. All professional bureaucracies are organized hierarchically, with accountability upwards to a superior, and ultimately to the relevant minister, and through the minister to parliament. But do not civil servants in a democracy also have a *direct* responsibility to the law, to parliament and to the public, which may on occasion transcend their accountability to a superior? What if the instructions they receive involve a breach of the law, the deception of parliament, or an infringement of the rights of clients of the service they are providing? Such examples demonstrate the possibility of a clear conflict between a bureaucratic and a democratic principle of accountability.

Recruitment of public servants

A final issue about the civil service in a democracy concerns its pattern of recruitment. Quality of entrants is typically secured by competitive selection from those with higher education or relevant professional training and expertise, independently of any party allegiance. However, while this ensures a certain intellectual exclusivity to recruitment, it is also important that it not be socially exclusive. The public service in a democracy should both be, and be seen to be, fairly representative of the main groups within society. And the principle of political equality requires that access to public appointment be equally open to all, regardless of which social group they belong to. This means that anti-discrimination and equal-opportunities policies should be effective within the education system as well as in recruitment to the civil service itself.

58. What contribution can individual citizens make to accountable government?

In a democratic system, individual citizens have important avenues of redress against government officials in the event of damage to their interests through unlawful decisions or maladministration (neglect, delay, arbitrariness, etc.). For decisions taken beyond government's legally defined powers, there is redress through the courts. In cases of maladministration there is the possibility of rectification through appeal to the constituent's elected representative, or through the office of an ombudsman, who has specific responsibility for assessing the validity of individual grievances against executive decision. Most recently developed has been the institution of the 'citizen's charter', whereby people are compensated for specific failures of a government service to meet designated standards of delivery. All these can be seen as examples of individual accountability, initiated by an aggrieved person, as opposed to the other more corporate forms of accountability already discussed (see question 51). They serve as an important reminder that the chief customer for government services is the public at large, and that the ultimate focus for the processes of legal, political and financial accountability of government are the citizens themselves.

THEY MAY NOT BE THE FIRST IN THEIR CLASS, BUT IN CIVICS, THEY'RE THE BEST!

59. How can the military remain accountable to citizens?

In long-established democracies, with a well-understood and carefully protected separation between political and military decisions, this hardly seems a major problem, except in occasional borderline disputes over weapons procurement, manning levels or conditions of service in the armed forces. In recently established democracies, on the other hand, which may have experienced a history of coups d'etat, military rule, or military veto over the personnel or policy of government, the problem may come to seem much more acute. After all, the military everywhere have the physical and organizational *capacity* to depose elected politicians, to take over the government, and to subject the population at large to their rule. The question, therefore, is one of their *willingness* to do so, and how this can be discouraged.

Military coups

Maintaining military subordination to elected politicians is rarely just a question of training them in a non-political role, or keeping them satisfied with pay and status and advanced technical weaponry. Internal dissatisfaction within the armed forces may have been historically a contributory factor in coups d'etat, but has rarely been the decisive one. They have usually only taken over civilian government when there has been a deep and sustained crisis in the democratic order which the politicians have proved incapable of resolving: civil war, chronic inflation, breakdown of public order, flagrant and persistent political corruption. Military coups have also taken place to preempt parties with radical programmes, which have threatened the established order of things, from winning at the polls or exercising office. In either case there has been some failure in the consolidation of workable democratic institutions that has been the root cause, not some inherent character of the military as such.

Military rule

Military rule can at best, however, only provide a short-term palliative to society's problems, not a long-term solution. A decade or two ago it was fashionable to exalt the military as the chief agency of economic modernization and nation-building, in contrast to the corruption and divisiveness of democratic politics. Yet the armed forces are simply incapable of providing a source of legitimate authority for government. And their record in power is dismal. Closed and secretive government may merely conceal corruption, rather than reduce it, and has proved no basis for sound economic management; and the military in power have a record of human rights abuses which no system of open government could tolerate.

Democratic consolidation

There is no serious alternative to the long road of consolidating democratic institutions, constitutional government and the rule of law, with international support if need be; and of seeking to resolve major societal conflicts through the political means of negotiation and compromise. At the same time, more effective methods need to be developed, at both national and international levels, for identifying and punishing serious human rights abuses, especially those perpetrated by state personnel; and for instituting sanctions against those regimes that permit them. The establishment of the International Criminal Court in 2002 has been a major step in this direction (see question 28).

60. Is there any place for a secret service in a democracy?

Democracy is in principle antithetical to secrecy anywhere in government. However, democratic states have always found it necessary to mount covert operations to protect society against external threat, internal organized crime and conspiracy to subvert the democratic process itself. The problem with such operations is that the methods employed – surveillance, bugging, telephone-tapping, 'dirty tricks' of all kinds – constitute an infringement of individuals' human rights; and that, precisely because they are so secretive, they can readily cross the boundary of publicly justifiable targets to include political organizations and activities which are perfectly legal, but which happen to be troublesome to a particular government and its policies.

Political accountability

Everything therefore hangs on the issue of political control. It is not sufficient for security operations to be covered in the general accountability of the relevant minister or ministers to parliament. There needs to be a special committee of parliament, meeting as necessary in secret, to supervise such activities, and ensure that publicly justifiable guidelines are being adhered to. And the ombudsman should have the power to investigate complaints from individuals who have grounds for believing that their human rights are being infringed in the surveillance of perfectly legitimate activities.

61. What is the relation between local government and democracy?

Having a system of elected local government is important to the vitality of a democratic system for a number of reasons. It greatly expands the opportunities for taking part in public decision-making, and the number of those involved in it. Because it is locally based, it is much more responsive to the particularity of local needs and circumstances than national government can be. It allows for small-scale experiments in policy, which if successful can be copied elsewhere, including at national level. It provides a stepping stone for politicians to national office, and a political base for parties which have been defeated nationally. Finally, by limiting the concentration of power in the hands of central government, it adds a spatial dimension to the constitutional separation of powers. Each of these features on its own is significant; taken together, they make a strong case for elected local government.

Centralizing tendencies

However, in contemporary states there are powerful forces at work which encourage the centralization of political decision-making. There is the pressure from treasury departments seeking to control the overall level of public expenditure as an essential instrument of national economic management. There is the reluctance of national politicians to allow political opponents at local level to obstruct or dilute central policy initiatives. Then there are also the expectations of the public at large, which in an increasingly mobile society becomes intolerant of significant variations in the standards of service provision from one locality to the next. Equality of citizenship means equality in the standards of service; if this can only be achieved by substantial redistribution of resources between different areas, as well as by national regulation, then this considerably restricts the autonomy of local government, and the scope of local electoral choice.

Competing imperatives

There is no easy solution to these competing imperatives, nor one that is universally applicable. However, since the most powerful pressures today come from the direction of centralization, it is the interests of local government and locality that most stand in need of protection. At a minimum, this might require: a clear separation of functions between centre and locality that is intelligible to the electorate; sufficient powers and resources to carry out these functions according to local needs and circumstances, albeit within the framework of national regulations; adequate mechanisms of accountability to the local electorate; restraint upon central government from interference in the discretion of local authorities, if necessary enforceable through a constitutional court. At the end of the day, however, effective relations between centre and locality depend upon cooperation and a mutual recognition of respective spheres, rather than narrow legalism.

62. What is federalism and when might it be appropriate?

Federalism involves the division of a national territory into separate states, each with its own elected parliament and executive, and the right to legislate and raise taxes according to a constitutionally guaranteed division of powers between the individual states and the government at national level. Historically, federal states have come into being in a number of ways: through the amalgamation of previously sovereign states; through the granting of autonomy to regions or nations within a previously unitary state; through the settlement of an original founding convention. A typical division of functions between states or provinces and the national government will allocate education, welfare, social and cultural services to the former, while overall economic policy and issues of defence and foreign policy, including treaty negotiation, will be the preserve of the national government.

Regional differences

Federalism is usually desirable in large territorial states, which contain wide variations in culture and geography between their constituent regions. It offers a potential solution anywhere to demands for autonomy from culturally or ethnically distinct minorities living within the same geographical area, as an alternative to outright independence. Living 'semi-detached' may be preferable both to complete detachment and to continuous squabbling under the same roof. Many of the arguments advanced in favour of elected local government (see question 61) can be seen to apply with equal force to federal systems.

5. Democratic or Civil Society

63. What is civil society?

The idea of civil society as a necessary component of democracy is one that has become particularly emphasized as a result of the twentieth century experience of fascist and Communist dictatorships, both of which sought to incorporate and supervise all social institutions under the aegis of the state. The concept of civil society can be looked at from two different aspects: *negatively*, the idea that the reach of the state should be limited, so that it is prevented from controlling all social activity, penetrating all spheres of life, or absorbing all social initiative and talent; and *positively*, the idea of having many independent foci of self-organization within society, through which people can work collectively to solve their own problems, which can act as channels of popular opinion and pressure upon government, and which can serve as a protection against its encroachments.

Elements of civil society
Among the key elements of civil society are: a market economy (see question 9); independent media of communication (question 6); sources of expertise on all aspects of government policy which are independent of the state; above all, a flourishing network of voluntary associations in all areas of social life, through which people manage their own affairs. At different times and places various of these associations will assume a particular significance in the defence and promotion of democracy, whether it be trade unions, professional associations, women's groups, human rights and development organizations, self-help groups, religious bodies, or grass-roots organizations of any kind. In an environment of freedom of expression and association, such groupings will develop spontaneously, as people recognize the need for collective action to organize their affairs, or to defend and advance their interests.

They can also be encouraged, however, by public recognition, for example, of their consultative role in relevant areas of government policy.

64. Can civil associations be undemocratic?

The fact that the associations and institutions of civil society are independent, i.e. self-organizing and self-financing, means that they may have the power to modify or even frustrate particular aspects of government policy. The point where this becomes undemocratic is not always easy to define. Most democratically elected governments will consult and compromise with organized social interests, since this is an essential feature of government by consent. However, some interest groups have much more influence over government than others, by virtue of their organization, wealth or connections. Where this influence derives from large numbers, and a mass membership, it must be judged more democratic than where it derives from concentrations of wealth or power in the hands of a few. In addition, where the internal organization of such associations is itself democratic, such that their leaders can be seen to be genuinely representative of their membership, they deserve to be treated with greater seriousness than where they are not. Finally, a democratic society ought to acknowledge a special consultative place for organizations representing people who by virtue of social, economic or physical disability have difficulty in making their voice heard in the political process, and who would otherwise remain disempowered.

The paradox of external funding

In many new and emergent democracies, some of the most influential associations of civil society are only able to survive with financial assistance from abroad, given the paucity of the domestic resource base. While such financing can be an important means of democratic assistance, there is also something paradoxical about the idea of a self-organizing civil society being organized from outside. Although associations financed in this way should not be outlawed, they should nevertheless be required to meet strict requirements of transparency in funding and policy formulation.

And external donors should be careful to see that they are not markedly privileged in comparison with traditional or indigenous forms of association.

Government co-optation

A different concern, more pertinent to developed democracies, is the increasing practice of governments contracting the delivery of public services, such as housing and welfare services, to voluntary organizations in the charitable sector. While this practice may seem to be of mutual benefit, there is a danger that it can come to compromise the independence of such associations by setting their agendas from above, and blunting their advocacy role in relation to government policy. In many Western countries, more than 50 per cent of the income of the voluntary sector now comes from government through various channels.

65. Should economic institutions be internally democratic?

Many democrats have argued that the places in which people work are among the most important for determining the character of their lives, and that democratizing the workplace should therefore be a high priority for those seeking a truly democratic society. At a minimum, this means preventing any obstruction employers might impose on the self-organization of workers in trade unions, so that they can act collectively to defend or advance their living standards and conditions of work and employment. More ambitious aims include schemes of co-determination and profit-sharing, which give all employees some responsibility for, and commitment to, the success of the organization as a whole. Although it may be argued that such schemes make it more difficult for employers to dismiss workers, and to ensure labour discipline, there is considerable evidence to suggest that those firms do best in a modern economy which are able to encourage the creative energies of all their employees; and that this is best achieved by treating them as 'citizens' rather than 'subjects'. Democracy and 'efficiency', in other words, are not necessarily antithetical, though democratization of the workplace can be expected to generate pressures for moderating large discrepancies in pay and conditions between management and the shop floor.

Accountability of economic institutions

In a democratic society, economic institutions also have responsibilities to their local community, especially for their environmental impact. Just as citizens should have the right of redress against state institutions, if their interests are seriously damaged by their activities, so also should they against private firms, in the event of assignable damage to their health or physical well-being. Private economic institutions should therefore be expected to operate within an effective framework of legal regulation and environmental protection, such as that set out in the UN Global Compact (July 2000).

66. Does democracy require private property?

Besides the economic arguments for the institution of private property, in terms of its necessity to a market economy, there are also sound political arguments relating to its importance for sustaining political activity independent of the state. Private property, even where it is collectively rather than individually owned, can thus be seen as a central institution of civil society, and as a protection for political liberty.

Limits on private property

It does not follow, however, that every state intervention in private property rights should be resisted as a threat to individual freedom. The institution of private property is itself premised upon a socially recognized and enforced limitation of individual freedom. The exclusive use of any possession presupposes that the freedom of others to have access to it is restricted. The terms on which such freedom is denied must therefore be socially determined, and in principle be subject to legislative variation as circumstances themselves vary. In short, the use of property may be legitimately controlled by law, and its pattern of distribution may be a legitimate concern of public policy. Although the principle of private property, therefore, is important to democracy, it cannot be a 'natural' or 'absolute' right, but only on terms and within limits that are collectively agreed. Different countries will of course vary considerably in the rights and responsibilities which their legal systems accord to property ownership.

67. Is democracy compatible with economic inequality?

This question cannot be answered with a simple 'yes' or 'no', but is a matter of degree. The greater the economic inequalities in a society, the more difficult it becomes to have effective political equality, since accumulations of wealth can be used as a significant resource to determine political outcomes. In the most extreme cases, the wealthy will see the votes of the poor as a potential threat to their interests, which justifies them in manipulating or subverting the electoral process. On the other side, if the poor cannot see any prospect of improving their lot through democratic means, they will not find democracy worth supporting. Here it is not just a question of the quality of democracy, but of its sustainability in any form.

Minimizing political inequality

However, some degree of economic inequality may be both inevitable and justifiable in a market economy. The concern of democrats should be to minimize the political impact or significance of such inequalities. At one end of the scale, there should be strict legislation limiting the amount of money that can be spent on election campaigns by both parties and individual candidates; preventing concentrations of media ownership; and requiring disclosure of sources of funding for parties and public campaigning of all kinds.

Protecting human rights

At the other end of the scale, all citizens should be guaranteed those minimum necessities of life which are the condition for the exercise of any effective citizenship. Without the guarantee of basic economic and social rights, including education, health and a means of livelihood, people's capacity to take part in public life is severely impaired (see question 22).

68. Does democracy depend upon economic development?

There is considerable evidence that the prospects for sustaining democracy, without slipping back into authoritarian rule, are greater the more economically developed a country is. This is because of the effects that economic development has upon the character of the citizen body and the structure of civil society. With widespread literacy and education comes a more mature and informed electorate. With an expanded middle class, occupying a variety of technical and professional roles, there is greater resistance to paternalist or authoritarian forms of government. And the process of economic development enhances the complexity of civil society, and the variety of self-organizing groups and associations with the confidence to defend their independence against government encroachment.

Exceptions

It would be wrong, however, to conclude that democracy can only be sustained where there is a high level of economic development. There are examples of countries in all continents which have maintained open electoral competition and civil and political liberties over decades despite low levels of economic development as measured by per capita GNP (e.g. India, Jamaica, Botswana). Government policies to encourage universal literacy may be more important than the particular level of economic development. And what fledgling democracies need more than anything else is sustainable economic growth, from whatever level of development they start, so that different sections of society are able to share in improvement, and the intensity of distributional conflicts is moderated. The policies of the major international economic agencies, and of developed countries, can be a significant help or hindrance in this context.

Democracy fostering development

It is now generally accepted that economic development cannot be treated as a purely quantitative concept, to be measured, say, by GNP per head of population. It is also a qualitative concept, about the well-being of a population, to which considerations of income

distribution, and the distribution of state expenditure (as between health or education and the armed forces) are particularly relevant. Now, it so happens that these qualitative aspects of economic development are themselves dependent upon the character of the political regime, and the degree of its responsiveness to the population. Democratic electorates are more likely to demand policies which moderate the extremes of economic inequality, and support state spending on health, education and the physical infrastructure rather than on the military or prestige projects with little social utility. Moreover, an open and accountable regime will use public resources more efficiently than a closed or authoritarian one. It will also be one in which major scandals, such as widespread human rights abuses, environmental degradation, or famine, cannot survive undetected for years. The positive relationship between democracy, development and the protection of human rights was underlined in the final report of the UN World Summit in 2005.

69. Does religion help or hinder democracy?

This is another question to which there is no simple 'yes' or 'no' answer, since so much depends upon the context. It is not even possible to separate the great world faiths into hard and fast categories, such as those which support democracy, those which are neutral, and those whose effects are disabling to it, since all religions contain within them a variety of competing tendencies. Historically, examples can be found within all faiths of support for authoritarian government and also support for those resisting it, often at one and the same time.

Religion and the state
It can be argued that a hierarchically ordered religion, where believers accept without question the truths that are handed down from above, will be less conducive to the democratic spirit than one where matters of belief are subject to lively debate and interpretation among the faithful. More crucial for democracy than the question of internal organization, however, is the relationship

of a given religion to the state. The closer the link between them, the less likely it is that those who belong to a different faith will be treated as equal citizens, or that religious dissent will be allowed full public expression. In the extreme case, where the religious authorities regard the state as the divine instrument for fulfilling a religious mission on earth, politics can readily take on the character of a crusade in which members of other faiths are forced into line and persecuted, and all freedom of expression becomes stifled.

Religious toleration

It is from the painful historical experience of such oppressions, and of the civil wars and communal violence they have generated, that the idea of religious toleration has emerged. Even if we believe our religion to possess the final and exclusive truth, the cost of compelling others to accept it is simply too high in human terms to be sustainable in a world characterized by a pluralism of different faiths. Toleration does not mean abandoning our own convictions, or refraining from proselytizing others; it means according people the basic human dignity of letting them decide for themselves, even when that leads them to decide wrongly.

Minority religions

The most effective environment in which both tolerance and acceptance of diversity of religion or belief can be secured is one in which no religious faith is given a privileged position within the state. Such a state may act to support religious faiths in an even-handed way, through taxation or assistance for religious schooling. Toleration may even persist in a state which involves one religion in matters, say, of state ceremonial, where it forms the religion of the large majority. However, once the state seeks to impose the precepts of a majority religion on non-believers, it will inevitably come to abrogate the basic democratic freedoms of expression and association for those who dissent, including those within the majority religion itself. Here we may note the divergence between what the majority at a given moment may want, and what the conditions for the ongoing popular control of government and for political equality may require.

70. What is the relation between democracy and multiculturalism?

Given the intermingling of different peoples, races and faiths which is the norm for contemporary societies, all require constitutional arrangements which serve to protect minorities against systematic discrimination or oppression (see questions 10 and 26). Nothing fuels communal antagonism more surely than when exclusion from political office brings with it the experience of discrimination, disadvantage or oppression for one community or another, or the fear that it will do so. Beyond protective constitutional arrangements, however, a democratic society requires a set of dispositions distinctive from its members. As regards a majority community, it is important that they should exercise their freedom of expression in a way that does not gratuitously offend vulnerable minorities. As regards minorities, their concern to protect and develop their own distinctive identities and way of life should not involve infringing or diminishing the principles of a common citizenship that is equal for all.

The rise of the 'extreme right'

A distinctive phenomenon of the late 20th and early 21st century in a number of European countries has been the rise of extreme right-wing parties. These have an agenda that is hostile to the presence of immigrants and their descendants, and sees the fact of multiculturalism as a threat to their own primordial definition of 'nationhood'. Such parties have been able to garner considerable electoral support, especially in localities where an indigenous population feels that the character of its neighbourhood has been altered without their consent. Banning such parties is not an option in a democratic society, though laws against incitement to hatred may be used against particular individuals. The impact of such parties can only be minimized by a combination of socio-economic improvements which are seen to apply fairly to all groups, together with cross-community dialogue and education involving a whole range of community and political leaders at local and national levels. None of this can be achieved overnight.

71. How can a culture of democracy be fostered?

Democratic thinkers have always argued that the practice of working democratic institutions helps develop a democratic culture, for example through the incentive it gives people to become informed about the issues on which they will have to decide, and through the skills and attitudes fostered by political participation at every level. Opportunities for such participation, therefore, both in the formal political sphere, and in the associations and institutions of civil society, should be as widespread as possible.

A culture of tolerance

Besides a disposition for civic engagement, a democratic culture also embodies attitudes of tolerance towards those who are different, and respect for the rights of others. A societal commitment to protect human rights forms an essential component of democracy, and it is a special responsibility of associations of civil society, including political parties, religious bodies and social movements of all kinds, to help foster a human rights culture among their members.

Other agencies for strengthening a democratic culture

A democratic culture is also fostered in many other ways. The arts can be an important vehicle for democratic ideas and practice, for the reflective articulation of contemporary problems and discontents, and for the representation of a society to itself. Public ceremonies can be used to celebrate specifically democratic and popular moments in a country's history and its institutions. Above all, the media play a crucial role in political education in the widest sense: in enhancing the level of public information and awareness, in the critical assessment of government policy, and in providing a channel through which members of the public can communicate with one another.

72. What role can schools play in education for democracy?

Besides the development of individual skills and capacities, especially literacy, and the transmission of knowledge, schools play a significant part in the handing on of a society's cultures and traditions. They also have a role in the critical evaluation of those cultures, and of helping children understand their place in an interdependent world of many faiths and beliefs, as well as

fostering attitudes of tolerance towards those who are different. More specific training for democracy will include an understanding of the country's constitution and how it came to be developed; a practical knowledge of the rights and duties of citizenship; and an appreciation of human rights and their importance.

Practical learning

A democratic education involves not only the acquisition of knowledge, however. It is also fostered through the experience of debate on issues of current importance, of presenting arguments and listening to the views of others, and of sharing in collective decisions on matters affecting the life of the school and its community, e.g. through classroom assemblies, elected school councils, and so on. The respective ages which are appropriate for the acquisition of these different skills and areas of knowledge will obviously differ according to the country and the pattern of its education system. For a democracy to overlook them, however, for example because they are too 'political', would be to incur the risk of serious erosion of its popular base.

73. In what ways is the institution of the family relevant to democracy?

Historically, and in most societies still today, families have tended to be organized in such a way that women undertake the major responsibility for child rearing and childcare, looking after the home, and servicing the domestic needs of men. These domestic arrangements, which appear to be an essentially 'private' matter, have an important public significance: in limiting the time and energy women have available for public activities, and in defining the public role that is suitable for them to fulfil. To the extent that these arrangements, and the attitudes supporting them, persist, women will be denied equality of political opportunity, and the quality of democratic life will suffer through their absence. The public status of women can be enhanced, however, by appropriate government policies, and through influence exerted by women themselves, via women's organizations, self-help groups, etc. (see question 38).

Children and democracy

The family also has a public significance in the positive role it can play in assisting the development of future citizens. The childhood experience of being valued equally, of learning both to have a say in domestic affairs and to respect the voice of others, of understanding that the exercise of rights entails corresponding duties – these are learning processes that are important for the later exercise of democratic citizenship. It is also through the family that children first learn attitudes towards the wider community, and develop opinions about political affairs that may persist throughout their adult lives.

6. The Future of Democracy

74. What are the main challenges facing democracy today?

Many of the challenges which democracies currently face, such as those of managing multicultural societies, improving the political participation of women, making power properly accountable, minimizing corruption, and so on, have been discussed in the answers to previous questions. Here a number of challenges arising at the international level, which have preoccupied democratic thinkers and practitioners over the past decade, will be addressed. These include:

- the challenge of globalization and the loss of democratic power to international forces;
- how international assistance for development and democracy can be made to work;
- the threats posed by violence of all kinds to democracy and human security;
- how international institutions can be democratized;
- remedying the lack of democratic control over national governments' international policies.

The book will conclude by returning to the domestic level and posing a question that concerns every country: how political apathy can be overcome, and democracy be made relevant to the people.

75. In what ways does globalization challenge democracy?

'Globalization' is a widely used term which has a variety of meanings. In the economic sense, it indicates an irreversible process of liberalization and intensification of trans-border economic transactions, by which national economies and governments become much more vulnerable to decisions on trade, investment, financial flows and currency movements which are taken beyond the country's borders. At a wider level 'globalization' points to the increasing *interdependence* of global society, such that decisions taken by people and governments in one place affect what happens elsewhere – with respect to the environment, physical security, public health, immigration flows, criminal activity, tax evasion, and so on. Because these processes are beyond the reach of national governments, the effectiveness of democracy is diminished. What is the advantage of popular control over government, if governments themselves do not have the power to determine what really matters for the well-being of their citizens?

One-sided globalization

Although these processes of globalization affect all countries, they have a particularly detrimental effect on developing economies. While more powerful countries can protect some of their producers through subsidies and other protectionist measures, especially in the agricultural sector, producers in developing countries are impoverished through competition from below-cost imports and from declining prices in other commodity markets. In addition, these countries have very little influence when it comes to the international organizations that determine trade regimes, loan conditions and investment ratings, all of which are largely controlled by developed countries. Since prospects for democratic consolidation are positively affected by economic development, especially where it is evenly distributed, it must be a matter of concern that, as the United Nations Development Programme (UNDP) *Human Development Report 2005* records, sub-Saharan Africa and the former Communist countries between them had nearly 200 million more people living in poverty in 2001 than in 1990, while Latin America and the Middle East registered no progress.

A global culture of democracy

Against these negative features of economic globalization should be set the development over the past decade of a strong international culture supporting democratic values and encouraging democratic processes in most countries of the world. It is now much more difficult for a country which reverts to authoritarian rule to gain international support. And regional organizations such as the Council of Europe, the Organization of American States and the African Union are supportive of democracy and human rights in their respective regions of the world. Yet the impact of this broadly progressive global culture is offset by the economic processes mentioned above, which lead huge numbers of the poor to question what difference the arrival of democracy actually makes to their daily lives.

76. How can international assistance best help emergent democracies?

Aid from economically developed countries to assist the less developed ones is an established feature of the international system, and one on which many countries have come to rely for the maintenance of their social programmes. In 2000, the international community committed itself through the UN to an ambitious programme of Millennium Development Goals, which aim to eradicate extreme poverty and hunger in all countries, to achieve universal primary education, promote gender equality, provide access to clean water and sanitation, and combat the most infectious diseases, including HIV/AIDS, by 2015. The UNDP *Human Development Report 2005* concluded, on the basis of progress to date, that 'almost all the goals will be missed by most countries, some of them by epic margins'. Among the reasons given are not only that most developed countries have not fulfilled their commitments on aid, but that the value of the aid given is offset many times over by the negative effects of unfair trade regimes and the requirements of debt repayment.

Aid and 'political conditionality'
A further reason for concern over the attainment of the Millennium Development Goals is that the impact of aid is reduced through ineffective targeting and corruption in the recipient countries. It is for this reason that international donor agencies have sought to link aid to improvements in a country's governance, including greater transparency and accountability. This has formed part of a larger process on the part of Western governments of using

aid and trade links as a lever to promote democracy and human rights (so-called 'political conditionality'). Such linkage had some success in the 1990s in accelerating progress towards multi-party elections and preventing relapses into authoritarianism. Yet it has also become discredited because conditionality has been applied inconsistently, being subordinated to other foreign policy goals, and has encouraged merely token compliance. The set of countries where it has proved most successful have been the countries from the former Communist bloc seeking membership in the European Union. Here the economic benefits of joining the Union have given them a strong incentive to accept quite stringent criteria for progress in democracy and human rights, as a condition of membership.

Democracy assistance

The best way in which established democracies can help emergent ones is by offering training and disseminating good democratic practices. Developing democracies can be helped with the training of all kinds of public officials: election officers, parliamentary clerks, constitutional lawyers, financial controllers, members of the legislature, party officials, and so on. The dissemination of good practice is most fully developed in the fields of electoral competition, where international panels are a widely accepted device for assessing to what degree elections are free and fair; and in the field of human rights, where clear international standards exist for both the content and the procedures of human rights provisions. However, the establishment of standards of good practice could be extended to many other areas of the democratic process, including open and accountable government. In all these areas the performance of some developed democracies themselves may leave a good deal to be desired; and their assistance to others will be the more credible, the more they show themselves ready to improve their own processes to the level of best international practice.

Sovereignty and international intervention

Decades of research on democracy assistance have shown that external support for a country's transition and consolidation will only be effective in so far as there are already substantial popular forces pushing for democratic change internally. Democracy is not something that can simply be brought from outside. Particularly problematic in this context is the idea of imposing democracy on a country by force – promoting a people's self-determination through a systematic violation of it. The final statement of the 2005 World Summit explicitly links the value of democracy with 'due respect for sovereignty and the right of self-determination'. Certainly the international community is now prepared to endorse armed intervention in a country to prevent a major humanitarian crisis. But the criteria for infringing a country's sovereignty have to be very tightly drawn, and will include at least the following conditions: that such intervention should be a last resort; that it should have a clear prospect of preventing massive human suffering that cannot be averted by other means; and that it be done under the authority of the UN Security Council.

77. How can democracies manage threats to their security?

Most established democracies see the major threat to their security today as coming from international terrorism. Many developing democracies, however, face a much greater threat: that of domestic insurgency, civil war, and incursions by private armies, often sponsored from outside the territory, and sustained by international trade in arms and mineral resources. Whereas wars in the twentieth century were mainly wars between states, at the start of the twenty-first century most conflicts are within states, and most victims are civilians, threatened not only by direct violence but also collapsing food systems and the destruction of basic services. The concept of 'human security' refers to the protection required against all these types of threat. Although democracy cannot be sustained in the midst of violent conflict, or in the context of failed states, democratic processes and institutions can play a decisive part in post-conflict resolution (see question 14).

Terrorism and democracy
International terrorism poses a number of challenges to democracy. Most obvious is the physical threat to civilians. Another is the creation of a pervasive climate of fear, which can be used by governments to erode long-standing civil and political freedoms

through anti-terrorist legislation. A third threat is the further alienation of sections of the population who may be already marginalized, but whose cooperation may be needed for the provision of effective intelligence. All the evidence suggests that the attempt to combat the threat of terrorism through repressive legislation and the militarization of police functions can be counter-productive, especially if its deeper sources in discriminatory practices at home or insensitive international policies are not addressed.

78. Can and should international institutions be democratized?

If it is correct, as indicated in answer to question 75, that many of the decisions that matter for the well-being of a country's people have now escaped beyond the control of the national state, then is it possible to re-establish some control for people at an international level? This question has two sides to it. One side involves the question of how to create or consolidate those international institutions that regulate and control the global forces and economic transactions which so profoundly affect the destiny of nations. Such institutions already exist: in the economic sphere, the International Monetary Fund, the World Bank, the World Trade Organization; in the human rights sphere, the international covenants and their respective committees, and the recently founded International Criminal Court; at the wider level, the UN itself and its various agencies. Despite these, much international activity slips through any regulatory net, for example offshore banking and tax havens which increasingly deny countries enormous sums which could be devoted to public welfare; or the activities of trans-national corporations, which are not subject to human rights regimes, since only states can be signatories to the relevant international conventions.

The principle of democratization

If one issue is how to make international regulatory regimes more effective and comprehensive, the other is how the institutions involved might be democratized, and made subject to a measure of popular control. It is of course a feature of regulatory bodies even at the national level, such as central banks or judicial bodies, that they possess a measure of independence from direct political control, since this is seen as desirable for their effective operation. Yet it is ultimately a democratic political authority, typically a national parliament, which sets the legal framework within which such bodies operate, and the legal norms they are required to apply. Is it possible to replicate such democratic institutions of representation and accountability at the international level?

Two models of democratization

Proposals to democratize international institutions fall into two broad camps. The first holds that such institutions will necessarily be *inter-governmental*, that is, composed of representatives from national governments. In so far as national governments are themselves democratically elected, then their ministers or other governmental delegates will be representative of their peoples, and so too the international organizations collectively. What is needed for fuller democratization on this view is, first, that all international bodies should either give equal effective weight to all countries rather than be biased systematically towards the wealthy and powerful, or else that countries' representatives should have weighted voting power proportional to the size of their respective populations. Secondly, these national delegations will only be truly representative of their peoples to the extent that all countries' governments meet some basic criteria for democratic authorization through competitive election under universal suffrage.

Cosmopolitan democracy

A more radical approach to the democratization of international institutions sees their main problem as being their state-centred character; and their assumption that the only way people's interests can be represented internationally is through their national governments, rather than more directly. This perspective focuses on the different ways in which the concerns of the world's peoples might be articulated directly at the international level, whether as a complement or an alternative to representation through governments. The idea of 'cosmopolitan democracy' proposes a regime of global governance in which people can engage directly, as citizens of the world, rather than only as citizens of a particular country. Such an arrangement is already prefigured in the development of a global civil society: in the involvement of NGOs at the meetings of international organizations; in cross-national groupings of minority and indigenous peoples; in international congresses of municipalities; and so forth. More formal representation of people could be achieved through the institution of a World parliament or a people's assembly at the UN.

79. Can democracies control the international policies of their governments?

If, for the foreseeable future, people's representation in international organizations is likely to be through their governments, then an important issue is how to achieve a measure of democratic control and accountability in the international policy of governments. The standard means for the oversight of the government or executive is through a national parliament and its scrutiny committees. Yet parliaments have historically proved relatively weak in the oversight of foreign policy, since this is an area that national governments have treated as a matter of executive privilege. Such a position is no longer tenable in an era when so much that a government is involved with internationally has direct repercussions on domestic conditions and policies. Thus, for example, a developing country's parliament, which has responsibility for approving the national budget, may find that decisions over priorities are largely pre-empted by debt repayments, in deciding the terms and conditions of which it has had no involvement whatsoever. In a similar way, the parliament of a European country may find that its legislative discretion has been surrendered to ministerial decisions in the Council of the European Union, over which it has no control or oversight. In all countries, parliaments will be required to ratify treaties the terms of which their governments may have approved without any parliamentary involvement.

Ensuring parliamentary oversight

As elected representatives of the people, members of national parliaments have a responsibility to reclaim the international policy of governments as a matter for their legislative oversight. This can only be done if they give themselves the legal powers to require advance information on government negotiating positions, and in sufficient time; and the right to influence those positions through direct meetings with the relevant ministers and other officials. This applies equally to major initiatives in international policy which governments may take unilaterally, such as decisions on whether to commit the country's troops on missions abroad. Decisions of this gravity should properly be subject to discussion and possible veto by parliament as a whole.

80. How can democratic apathy be addressed?

It is appropriate to end a book of questions and answers on democracy with the most crucial question of all. If the people see no point in democracy, because it seems to have no relevance to their everyday lives and the situation in which they live them, they will not do anything to defend it, or take part in its processes. If

the choices they are offered at election time make no difference to them, because politicians lack the ability or the will to change anything in the direction people have voted; if politicians are more attentive to powerful interests and lobbies than to their constituents; if the basic civil and political rights are not sufficiently guaranteed to enable people to organize and campaign on public issues without fear; above all, if people have no power to affect their situation at the most local levels of the workplace and the neighbourhood; then democracy has become an empty shell, a form without any substance. The task facing democrats everywhere is how to strengthen the substance behind the form, and to make the principles of popular control and political equality more institutionally effective, whether it be in the democratization of a previously authoritarian regime, or in the renewal and deepening of democracies that are longer established.

Further Reading

1. Basic Concepts and Principles
Axtmann, R. (ed.). 2003. *Understanding Democratic Politics*. Sage Publications, London, Thousand Oaks, Calif., and New Delhi.
Beetham, D. 2005. *Democracy: a Beginner's Guide*. Oneworld Publications, Oxford.
Dahl, R. 1998. *On Democracy*. Yale University Press, New Haven and London.
Huntington, S. P. 1991. *The Third Wave*. University of Oklahoma Press, Norman and London.

2. Human Rights and Fundamental Freedoms
Levin, L. 2005. *Human Rights: Questions and Answers*. UNESCO, Paris.
Marks, S. and Clapham, A. 2005. *International Human Rights Lexicon*. Oxford University Press, Oxford and New York.
Smith, R. K.M. 2005. *Textbook on International Human Rights*. Oxford University Press, London and New York.

3. Free and Fair Elections
Catt, H. 1999. *Democracy in Practice*. Routledge, London and New York.
Goodwin-Gill, G. 1994. *Free and Fair Elections*. Inter-Parliamentary Union, Geneva.
Reynolds, A., Reilly, B. and Ellis, A. 2005. *Electoral System Design: the New International IDEA Handbook*. International Institute for Democracy and Electoral Assistance, Stockholm.

4. Open and Accountable Government
Beetham, D. 2006. *Parliament and Democracy in the Twenty-first Century: a Guide to Good Practice*. Inter-Parliamentary Union, Geneva.
Schedler, A., Diamond, L., and Plattner, M. (eds). 1999. *The Self-Restraining State: Power and Accountability in the New Democracies*. Lynne Rienner, Boulder, Col.
UNDP. 2002. *Human Development Report 2002: Deepening Democracy in a Fragmented World*. Oxford University Press, New York and Oxford.

5. Democratic or Civil Society
Burnell, P. and Calvert, P. (eds). 2004. *Civil Society in Democratization*. Frank Cass, London and Portland, Ore.
Kaviraj, S. and Khilnani, S. (eds). 2001. *Civil Society: History and Possibilities*. Cambridge University Press, Cambridge and New York.
Sen, A. 1999. *Development as Freedom*. Oxford University Press, Oxford and New York.

6. The Future of Democracy
Held, D. 2004. *Global Compact*. Polity Press, Cambridge and Malden, Mass.
Holden, B. (ed.). 2000. *Global Democracy: Key Debates*. Routledge, London and New York.
Stiglitz, J. 2002. *Globalization and its Discontents*. Allen Lane, London and New York.

International Websites

Amnesty International:	www.amnesty.org
Article 19 Global Campaign against Censorship:	www.article19.org
Freedom House:	www.freedomhouse.org
Human Rights Watch:	www.hrw.org
International Foundation for Election Systems:	www.ifes.org
International Institute for Democracy and Electoral Assistance (IDEA):	www.idea.int
Inter-Parliamentary Union:	www.ipu.org
Minority Rights Group International:	www.minorityrights.org
Office of the United Nations High Commissioner for Human Rights:	www.ohchr.org
Open Democracy:	www.opendemocracy.net
Transparency International:	www.transparency.org
United Nations Development Programme:	www.undp.org
United Nations Educational, Scientific and Cultural Organization:	www.unesco.org